THE
CONSERVATIVE
MOVEMENT

SOCIAL MOVEMENTS PAST AND PRESENT

Irwin T. Sanders, Editor

THE
CONSERVATIVE
MOVEMENT

Paul Gottfried
and
Thomas Fleming

Twayne Publishers • Boston
A Division of G.K. Hall & Co.

The Conservative Movement
Paul Gottfried and Thomas Fleming

Copyright 1988 by Paul Gottfried and Thomas Fleming
All rights reserved.
Published by Twayne Publishers
A Division of G.K. Hall & Co.
70 Lincoln Street, Boston, Massachusetts 02111

Copyediting supervised by Lewis DeSimone
Book production by Janet Zietowski
Typeset by Compset, Inc., of Beverly, Massachusetts

Printed on permanent/durable acid free paper
and bound in the United States of America

Library of Congress Cataloging-in-Publication Data
Gottfried, Paul.
The conservative movement / Paul Gottfried and Thomas Fleming.
    p.   cm.—(Social movements past and present)
Bibliography: p.
Includes index.
ISBN 0-8057-9723-8 (alk. paper).
ISBN 0-8057-9724-6 (pbk. : alk. paper)
1. Conservatism—United States.   2. United States—Politics and
government—1945–   I. Fleming, Thomas, 1945–
II. Title.   III. Series.
JA84.U5G67 1988
320.5′2—dc19
87-18129
CIP

Contents

About the Authors

Paul Gottfried is a senior editor of the journal *The World and I* and editor in chief of *Continuity: A Journal of History.* He is the author of *Conservative Millenarians: The Romantic Experience in Bavaria, Arthur Schopenhauer and the Heritage of European Pessimism, The Search for Historical Meaning,* and numerous essays on social and intellectual history. He is also a former Guggenheim Fellow and former professor of history at Rockford College.

He and his wife and five children reside in North Bethesda, Maryland.

Thomas Fleming is the editor of *Chronicles: A Magazine of American Culture* and executive secretary of the Ingersoll Prizes. He has taught Greek and Latin at Miami University (Ohio) and the College of Charleston. He is the founding editor of *Southern Partisan,* and his essays and reviews on literature and politics have appeared in classical journals, magazines, and newspapers. He is the author of *The Politics of Human Nature* (1988).

With his wife and four children, he lives in Rockford, Illinois.

Preface

This book treats the American Right primarily as a political movement—or, more properly speaking, as a series of movements—since World War II. The preparation of this study required the making of far-reaching structural decisions. In order to focus on postwar conservative movements, we limited discussion of prewar American conservatism to a few scattered pages. Even less attention is given to the European and classical antecedents of modern conservatism. These thematic decisions, though necessary, were, for us, painful because of our scholarly interest in classical civilization and in European thought. Many of the ideas in this book came out of conversations we held in the course of translating Greek philosophy. The shades of Plato and Aristotle were present to inspire us, even where they are not acknowledged in the text.

Yet one conclusion that may be drawn from this book is the increasing irrelevance of prewar, especially non-American, traditionalist thinking for the postwar Right. A distinctive feature of the contemporary American Right is its emphasis on progress: moving beyond the past toward a future of unlimited material opportunity and social improvement.

One prominent conservative congressman, Newt Gingrich, added a revealing subtitle to his book *Window of Opportunity,* namely, "A Blueprint for the Future." He even went so far as to invite a leading science-fiction writer to compose a preface. While conservatives may well take a justifiable pride in their willingness to face the future, some of them, at least, may have less justification for describing themselves as conservative. Whereas the older traditional Right, particularly in Europe, looked backward for its ideals and values, the politics of nostalgia has been in decline on the American Right for at least the last two decades. The Moral Majority may deplore the breakdown of the family, but its leader, the Reverend Jerry Falwell, also praises the advances in civil rights and sexual equality that have taken place during the last generation. Moral Majoritarians are careful to invoke the spirit of social progress and to confine their attacks to "extremists" who carry change too far. Granted, a more thoroughgoing antimodernism can still be found on the American Right—for example, among disciples of Russell Kirk and among those of the Southern Agrarians—but its impact on American conservative politics at this time continues to be negligible.

In November 1985 the editors of *Commentary* magazine invited more than thirty recognizably conservative, neoconservative, and center-left intellectuals to respond to questions about American developments since 1945. The majority of the respondents lamented the continued power and oppressive policies of the Soviet Union, but they maintained that Americans had made social as well as economic progress since World War II. Most of the writers depicted the America of 1945 as a country tainted with racial and religious bigotry. Among the achievements since then, as one contributor put it, "[t]he Southern part of the U.S. has seen and shaken off its medieval torpor and, if you happen to have been black, cruelty."[1] Peter L. Berger, a leading sociologist of religion and a frequent contributor to conservative journals, was perhaps the most emphatic in celebrating the American success story since 1945. Berger extolled the "gigantic political efforts to ensure that no group within it [America] is excluded from the cornucopia of industrial capitalism" and marveled at how "racial discrimination was abolished in the span of a few years."[2] Looking toward a future of further improvements, he proposed "constructing a specifically American version of the welfare state" without the kind of officialdom that has accompanied similar projects in Europe. Less optimistic voices were raised in the symposium; a few contributors, most notably Robert Nisbet, were even vitriolic in decrying what they saw as social decay in America. There were also critical remarks about crime in the streets and eroded educational standards mixed in with the hymn to contemporary America. But something notably absent from most of the responses was that skepticism about progress that in earlier generations characterized the thought of intellectuals identified as conservatives.

This raises the question of an editorial decision that was willy-nilly thrust on us, deciding who is—or who is not—a conservative. There are sound philosophical criteria that might be used to exclude obvious non-conservatives. No one, except in an academic debate or as a member of the extreme Left, would call Gloria Steinem and George McGovern conservatives. Both favor extensive economic redistribution and speak more positively of socialist than capitalist or quasi-capitalist economies. But even more critical than their policy prescriptions is their theoretical point of departure. They favor a state-controlled economy, because they believe it can implement more easily than the free market the overriding good of a class- and gender-free society. True conservatives do not object to social and sexual distinctions, certainly not on principle. One is justified in making this assertion even though there are different types of conservatives, ranging from religious traditionalists to almost thoroughgoing skeptics.

Whatever the differences that characterize their various schools of thought, conservatives, as much as Leftists, are united by a distinctive approach to reality—particularly nature. For the Left, the concept "nature" suggests infinite plasticity; for the Right, by contrast, it is something fixed, and even normative. One sees nature as a material condition to be adapted to the "rational" goals of social planners; the other views it as a source of unchanging truth in a world otherwise in flux. This sense of human limitation is an important link between Old Right "reactionaries" and those neoconservatives who have effectively documented the "unintended consequences" of many social programs. In the end, it may also be a set of attitudes, not rigorously developed views, that define conservatives; adherence to these attitudes was once deemed essential to conservative self-identification.

One such attitude is a view of history as "the funded wisdom of the past," in the phrase of the postwar conservative Will Herberg. Conservatives view history not as a burdensome legacy but as a cumulative and morally binding set of guidelines for life in the present. Robert Nisbet, the conservative social theorist, makes this point with eloquent clarity: "Whereas the progressive rationalists see the present as the beginning of the future, the true way—the conservative way—is to see it as the latest point reached by the past in a continuous, seamless growth." Furthermore, "From the conservative point of view social reality was best understood through a historical approach. We cannot know where we are, much less where we are going, until we know where we have been."[3] For the authentic conservative, history must remain a constant point of orientation for the individual as well as the store of received assumptions needed to maintain a decent social existence.

Another conservative attitude is Aristotelian. In the *Politics,* Aristotle discusses the need for differentiated social roles and responsibilities. The philosopher stresses the differing ways in which the head of the household deals with his wife, children, and servants. The master and each member of the household must acquire his (or her) own form of excellence in order to advance the good of the whole, upon which the individual good remains dependent. Aristotle asserts that contrary to Socrates "there are not simply courage and justice, but two different types: the courage of commanders and the courage of subordinates, and the same applies to other things."[4] Aristotle goes on to chide those who deceive themselves by interpreting "excellence in general as a sound state of mind or a manner of acting well." Far better, it seems to him, "to enumerate forms of excellence as a means of defining it."

Our choice of authorities is certainly not arbitrary. Aristotle, who classified governments and social groupings as well as flora, fauna, and the rules of logical discourse, exemplified conservative attitudes. He considered monarchy, aristocracy, and limited democracies all to be forms of government that satisfied man's rational, material, and social needs, and he saw the weaknesses and strengths of each without being a political reductionist. He also emphasized the need for governments to be suitable to the specific historic conditions of peoples. Aristotle recognized that a well-ordered society protected an ascending order of good through the institutionalization of rank. One who commanded was expected to show greater excellence of mind than one who served. And though not all social and familial hierarchies corresponded to the differential capacities of their individual members, ascribed ranks were not purely capricious. There were inherent differences between men and women, parents and children, and even masters and servants that make one group more suitable for rule than another.[5] Moreover, the operation of custom (to which Aristotle assigned greater social and moral significance than law) ensured the acceptance and exercise of responsibility by members of the political community as well as by those of the household. Not only Aristotle, but also Plato, Cicero, Montesquieu, Edmund Burke, and Alexis de Tocqueville exalted custom as the protector of social morality. All of them suggested what finally became a conservative truism: we learn to be good not so much through reasoning as through the learning of ancestral ways.

Related to the conservatives' sense of order is a high regard for civility. Edmund Burke (and his American disciples) lamented the death of chivalry, but in the 1960s the progressive incivility on college campuses forced many respectable liberals to acknowledge their conservative inclinations. In a time of crisis, people are forced to choose a position on one side or the other of the barricades. Those who became neoconservatives opted for civility.

Another conservative characteristic—even among statist counterrevolutionaries—is a high regard for personal autonomy, or, in a word, liberty. King Charles I of England went to his execution proclaiming himself the defender of liberty and "the martyr of the people." If there is a common thread that runs through the pages of *National Review* (Old Right), *Conservative Digest* (New Right), *Public Interest* (neoconservative), *Reason* (libertarian, and *New American* (John Birch Society), it is the idea of defending personal liberty against the growing power of an increasingly socialist state. Conservatives quarrel over which freedoms take precedence over others, but none would endorse the Leftist exaltation of the state as the source of public virtue.

We are not seeking to justify conservative thinking against its critics. It may be true that conservatives have sometimes disregarded the costs of maintaining a traditional society; they may well be guilty of turning custom or liberty into idols to which greater goods have been sacrificed. Such recriminations are beside the point if the stated goal is to provide a workable description of an ideal conservative. The theoretical conservative welcomes human and social diversity. According to one French critic of the Left, he also rejects "abstract, universal egalitarianism" as incompatible with what he knows—or believes—about human nature.[6] This conservative distaste for abstract universalisms came out very clearly in the response that a founder of *National Review,* James Burnham, made in 1972 to Peter Berger's call for a "conservative humanism": "Conservatism can be considered humanist only if humanism is interpreted to mean a concern with the interests and well-being not of abstract Man or Mankind, but of existential Man, historical Man, or of actual men as they actually exist in space and time."[7]

Burnham was not inventing his own political doctrines but paraphrasing Edmund Burke, a recognized father of European conservatism who had defended the "liberties of an Englishman" against the French Revolution's Rights of Man. Like Burke and Burnham, theoretical conservatives believe in historic, not human, rights and view men in the context of established communities. Man's "natural" condition is not to be *apolis,* without communal identity; Aristotle taught that only gods or beasts could exist in such anarchy. This Aristotelian view of man's social and historic nature pervades the works of recognized European conservatives. It can also be discovered in the self-declared European liberal Friedrich Hayek, and in American conservative writings well into the 1960s. Significantly, what have been described as conservative attitudes may no longer be relevant to what are now the dominant tendencies in American conservatism.

This raises the methodological question: Should we abandon the theoretical definition in order to treat as conservatives those who are conventionally identified as such? Up to a point, we must work within a
relative frame of reference. In a relative sense, for example, S.M. Lipset, Daniel Bell, and Sidney Hook, all strongly anticommunist and moderate social democrats, are politically more conservative than George
McGovern and Gloria Steinem; the latter advocate radical social reforms
and avoid at all costs making anticommunist remarks. This judgment can
be made without assuming any kinship between Sidney Hook and Edmund Burke or between Daniel Bell and James Burnham, although such
connections are not always hard to locate. Moreover, some of our subjects may be considered conservative in the purely descriptive sense of
defending the political-economic status quo. Inasmuch as they criticize
attempts to carry income redistribution or social engineering beyond
points already reached, they become the party of resistance to further
change. Presentism, as viewed by reformers, has conservative effects,
even if it happens to support a society radically altered by earlier change.

It may be justified to exclude from our discussion elements of the lu-
natic Right, more specifically the American Nazi party, the Ku Klux Klan,
the Liberty Lobby, and the most recent practitioners of white racist violence (mostly from the mountain states), the Posse Comitatus. The
combined impact of these groups on postwar conservative politics and
thinking has been at most negligible. Main-line conservative publications,
starting with *National Review,* have spared no effort in condemning the
politics of violence and racial hostility.

It may also be redundant to devote more than a few words to the John
Birch Society and to Robert Welch, its founder. Although Birchers have
not generally preached violence or racism (one of their early leaders was
George Schuyler, a black journalist), their conspiratorial view of the
spread of communism, which led some Birchers, including Welch, into
accusing Dwight Eisenhower of being a conscious Communist agent,
caused them to become marginalized within the postwar conservative
movement. By the late sixties, William F. Buckley, Jr., Russell Kirk, and
other conservative celebrities were openly contemptuous of both Welch
and his followers. By the mid-seventies, John Birch membership rolls
numbered no more than in the low thousands. The claim made by Welch
at that time of having 80,000 members whose names he would not di-
vulge met with understandable skepticism. It was perhaps Kirk who best
expressed the mainstream conservative attitude of amused scorn for the
John Birch Society when he responded to Welch's charge against the
president: "Eisenhower isn't a Communist—he's a golfer!"[8]

We have chosen, in practice, to employ a relative and structural definition of conservatism, ascribing that designation to those who answer it and who are associated with it by others. But this choice may also lead to a misunderstanding, namely, taking a policy that is objectionable to the political Left for an expression of conservative belief. A specific illustration may help underline this problem. The American Right since the 1950s has steadily opposed Soviet expansion and the Soviet regime generally. This anti-Soviet stand is apparent whether one looks at the *National Review* of the late fifties or *Commentary* and the *New Republic* during the 1980s. Yet, as one proceeds from the anti-Soviet polemics of one generation on to those of another, a thematic change becomes obvious. The older conservative writings express hostility toward communism as the enemy of the Western religious heritage, of historic nationalities, and of metaphysical as well as political freedoms. The recent anticommunist writings rest on the stated or implicit assumption that American democracy with its mixed economy is the supreme human good. Articles in *Commentary* and other neoconservative publications, like Michael Ledeen's "How to Support the Democratic Revolution" (March 1985), call for redoubled American efforts on behalf of exporting our democratic way of life. Part of the change, we are told, is dictated by expediency. It is, at the very least, rhetorically necessary for conservatives to distance themselves from anticommunist military dictators. Apart from this political pragmatism, we are led to believe that spreading democratic values is at the heart of our national heritage. The National Endowment for Democracy, which has been set up and funded by the Reagan administration, promotes global democracy. The model that the advocates of the democratic revolution wish to advertise or, in some cases, impose is as far removed from a traditionalist worldview as from Marxist-Leninism: It is secularist, politically and sexually egalitarian, and opposed to pure capitalism as well as pure socialism.

Eric von Kuehnelt-Leddihn, an Austrian classical liberal and a cofounder of *National Review,* seemed utterly mystified when he recently discovered how closely American conservatism had become identified with democratic equality. "Do not forget," he warned an interviewer from the *Washington Times,* "that democracy, *in itself,* by its very principle, is totalitarian. It is the politicization of the whole nation."[9]

One explanation for this crusade may lie in the desperate response of anticommunist conservatives faced by the growing unpopularity of the Cold War and the identification, particularly in the media, of Marxist revolution with social justice. But this approach scarcely applies to every case. Among the advocates of the democratic revolution are those who still associate themselves with the anticommunist democratic Left; indeed, some representatives of this position, notably Jeane Kirkpatrick, are today admired everywhere on the political Right. Besides, the democratic globalism that members of the current Right preach against the Communists creates geopolitical imperatives different from those advocated by the older postwar Right. The older conservatives sought to contain and, where possible, push back the Soviets and their clients; the democratic globalists hope to impose their own vision of progress on both allies and enemies.

The current anticommunists may also have gained control over the issue of anticommunism at the expense of the older Right. Critics of democratic globalism have come from the ranks of theoretical conservatives as well as from elsewhere. In 1972 James Burnham noted that there were those still in transition from liberal beliefs who rejected part of their old doctrines but clung to "the emotional gestalt of liberalism, the liberal sensitivity, and temperament." Such people typically insisted on applying universal yardsticks to foreign policy and sought to substitute their own conception of "compassion, kindliness, love and brotherhood" for "those virtues indispensable to organized human society." Against what he considered doctrinaire universalist politics, Burnham appealed to the ancient values of the city: "Courage, duty, discipline, and especially self-discipline, loyalty, endurance, yes patriotism."[10]

The historian and historical conservative John Lukacs has ridiculed postwar American conservatives for believing that America's destiny is to "make the world safe for democracy." Lukacs sees the American Right as the victim of its own *American* "ideas of progress and modernism and American exceptionalism at the expense of the kind of historical understanding that had been enunciated by Burke."[11] Lukacs identifies the Right's global anticommunism with Woodrow Wilson's vision of a world transformed by American democracy. This identification may be far more accurately applied to the democratic globalism of the 1980s than to the Cold War anticommunism of the 1950s. Lukacs himself, in *Outgrowing Democracy,* gives at least two views (neither of them flattering) of the postwar conservative movement: one of primarily Midwestern, Anglophobe politicians and their intellectual spokesmen who glorified power politics; and the other of democratic globalists seeking to convert the world to "the American way of life," but ignoring the threat posed by unprotected borders being overrun by Third World flotsam.[12]

Although both pictures contain caricatures, they do represent phases in the evolving postwar Right. The democratic globalists of the eighties have little in common with the more traditional anticommunists of the fifties and sixties, save for the "anticommunist" label. James Burnham's *Suicide of the West* was a work that American conservative journals and the Conservative Book Club lavishly praised in the mid-sixties. In it Burnham attacked the universalist, egalitarian premises of the intellectual-journalistic community. He failed to see that the "liberal" premises he despised would eventually provide the substance of a transformed American Right. Like other traditional conservatives, Burnham underestimated the anticommunism of those he considered democratic ideologues. Nor did he and his colleagues twenty-five years ago foresee a fateful irony, that those whom they blamed for the self-destruction of the West would soon, in some cases, be rallying anticommunists in the name of democratic universalism.

If, as some would have it, the essence of conservatism is the preservation of a status quo, then it is perfectly natural that its principles should always be in flux; it is far more changeable than liberalism or Marxism, both of which possess something like an agenda. In this sense, it is possible to regard conservatism as a series of trenches dug in defense of last year's revolution. While we believe there is more than stupid tenacity to conservative politics, it is, nonetheless, an important element. The forty years of postwar conservative thought might well be summed up by inverting a common French proverb: the more things stay the same, the more they change.

Many people have lent their assistance to the authors in preparing this work. Special thanks go to Robert Nisbet, John Howard, Michael Warder and Allan Carlson for reading parts of the manuscript and offering detailed suggestions and critical comments, to Cynthia Calvert for painstakingly correcting the text, to Anita Fedora for typing it under pressure, to Jean Avery for helping to prepare an early version, to LeAnn Manning for handling a thousand vexing details, and to our wives, who endured the disruptions of everyday living and the extended political monologues that inevitably accompany a work of this type.

Chapter One

Forming a Worldview:
Conservatism in the Fifties

Paradise Lost

The postwar conservative movement took shape as a growing response to unwelcome change. One change that conservatives protested with particular vehemence was the growth of an American welfare state, particularly since the New Deal. George Nash, the leading historian of American conservatism, has described the horror felt by many Americans at the end of World War II when they considered both the erosion of economic freedom at home and the inroads of communism and socialism in Europe. Finding in America a "superstate, a partially controlled economy, millions of conscripts under arms and widespread fears of reversion to depression once demobilization set in," American opponents of the welfare state were even more "stunned" when in the summer of 1945 the English installed a socialist government. Nash argues convincingly that the sense of lost freedom within the English-speaking world was central to postwar conservatism.[1]

The Libertarian Response

The first strain that appeared in this movement was both libertarian and individualist. In February 1945, the historian Mortimer Smith, writing in *Christian Century,* lamented that "old-fashioned liberalism . . . is

1

all but dead in our century," a casualty of government social planning accelerated by war.[2] On 2 August the *New York Times* reported the manner in which the newly elected Labour government had entered Parliament on the preceding day. The exultant Labourites sang the "Red Flag" and other songs that the revolutionary Left had popularized in the 1930s.[3]

Postwar libertarians benefited from their contact with members of the Austrian School of Economics, which had been criticizing socialist programs and Marxian views of capitalism since the 1870s. The Austrian economist Friedrich von Hayek provided his American admirers with an extraordinary polemical weapon in his *The Road to Serfdom,* published in 1944. An ethical defense of free enterprise, Hayek's work noted both the socialist impulse of fascism and the antiliberal character of the modern planned economy. To the chagrin of English Labourites (he wrote his book as an exile from the Nazis in England) and of American New Dealers (whom he came to know at the University of Chicago after the war), Hayek interpreted economic planning and material redistribution as a retreat from the age of individual liberty. This age had dawned upon the West with the passing of medieval authority. The socialists, under the guise of guaranteeing equality, were setting mankind back on the road to serfdom.

The Road to Serfdom brought fame to Hayek. *Reader's Digest* serialized his work, which was also selected as a Book-of-the-Month Club offering. In 1954, the Harvard historian H. Stuart Hughes, a man of the socialist Left, observed in retrospect, "The publication ten years ago of Friedrich Hayek's *The Road to Serfdom* was a major event in the intellectual history of the United States."[4] Hughes attributed the restored prestige of free market thought in the fifties largely to Hayek's moral defense of capitalism. The attempt to revitalize the ideal of a free society, which Hayek so ardently encouraged, found expression on the international level with the creation of the Mt. Pelerin Society in 1949. A yearly gathering of classical liberal economists and social philosophers, it eventually numbered princes and statesmen among its guests and members. Ludwig Erhardt, chancellor of the Federal Republic of Germany, for example, was long associated with this partial brainchild of Hayek's.[5]

Libertarian critics of the welfare state were conspicuous in laying the intellectual foundations of a postwar conservative movement. Among these critics were Frank Chodorov, founder of Intercollegiate Society of Individualists, a group that from 1953 on published and funded libertarian and other conservative scholarship; Albert Jay Nock, who wrote scathingly against the modern state and was the original editor of the individualist periodical the *Freeman*; Milton Friedman and Frank H. Knight, both professors of economics at the University of Chicago; and those members of the Austrian School who had emigrated to America, most notably Hayek and Ludwig von Mises. William A. Rusher, publisher of *National Review* and cofounder of the Draft Goldwater Campaign, recalls his own excited reaction when he encountered Hayek's writings as a Wall Street attorney in the early 1950s. Like other groping conservatives of the time, Rusher found his opposition to social planning strengthened even more when he turned to the *Freeman,* which three of Hayek's disciples, John Chamberlain, Henry Hazlitt, and Suzanne LaFollette, had reestablished in 1950. Rusher believed that the *Freeman* was "a sort of journalistic John the Baptist" for *National Review,* which first appeared in November 1955.[6] Between the two publications there were obvious lines of continuity. The Nockean editors of the *Freeman* eventually joined the staff of what became the more widely circulated, anticollectivist periodical. Their antistatist, individualist creed remained essential to the moral teachings of *National Review*—and was then imperfectly transferred to the conservative politics of the 1960s.

Two other libertarian journals furnished the staff and many of the early contributors to Buckley's enterprise. One was the *American Mercury,* which H. L. Mencken founded, primarily as a literary and cultural journal, in January 1924. In the early fifties, under the editorship of William Bradford Huie, the *American Mercury* entered its last phase as an intellectually serious publication, presenting feisty criticism of the welfare state in lively prose. Max Eastman, John Dos Passos, James Burnham, Frank S. Meyer, and the young Buckley all wrote frequently for the *American Mercury* before the birth of *National Review. Human Events,* organized in 1944, was another libertarian periodical that channeled talent into the incipient *National Review.* Although originally designed to report and interpret foreign policy from Washington, D.C., *Human Events* also came to focus on economic and cultural issues. Among its editors and regular contributors were Felix Morley, an educator who wrote on educational issues, and John Chamberlain, who was also associated with the *Wall Street Journal* and the *Freeman.* In February 1955 Buckley observed in a letter to Eastman that there were only three journals of value on the Right: the *Freeman,* the *American Mercury,* and *Human Events.*[7] While the *National Review* was going to dominate the world of conservative letters, absorbing the editorial staffs of other publications and going between 1955 and 1965 from 30,000 to well over 100,000 subscribers, it also eclipsed its predecessors. *Human Events* continued to publish, but only as a weekly news report for conservatives. The *Freeman* also survived but with fewer readers than before; *American Mercury* went under—after lurching briefly to the far Right.[8]

Red Scare

Anticommunism, together with opposition to Soviet imperialism, was another force that shaped postwar conservative thinking. The first attempt at making conservatism a political movement came during the early phases of the cold war. Thinkers who had once been on the far Left, like James Burnham, Frank S. Meyer, and Whittaker Chambers, tried to make the American people aware of the danger of Soviet subversion. Whittaker Chambers's *Witness,* the graphic account of its author's transformation from a Communist agent into a self-declared counterrevolutionary, both inspired and galvanized American anticommunists. Chambers's understanding of his role in exposing Alger Hiss, a former State Department official, as a Soviet spy in 1948, was presented in stark, apocalyptic terms. Chambers saw himself participating in a struggle between "the two irreconcilable faiths of our time—Freedom and Communism." The cause of freedom, he thought, was doomed without "faith in God."[9] Such faith distinguished the traditional Western conception of freedom from the Promethean view, "the vision of man's mind displacing God as the creative intelligence of the world," that underlay the Communist system of servitude.

The anticommunism expressed by young conservative intellectuals in the 1950s had a metaphysical dimension already present in Chambers's writings. This metaphysical anticommunism was evident in the way that conservative intellectuals rose to the defense of Senator Joseph McCarthy between 1950 and 1954. McCarthy gained national attention after making charges against alleged Communists in the State Department and elsewhere in the government. His sweeping accusations and his often abrasive exchanges with the press made him rapidly into a controversial figure. By 1954 he fell out with members of his own party and with the military, which he accused of harboring Communist sympathizers.

There were compelling historical reasons for the widespread support McCarthy commanded as a Senate investigator up to (and even after) the time the Senate censured him on 30 July 1954. Most attempts by his liberal critics to identify his following largely or exclusively with "reactionary" minorities—such as anti-Eastern populists, Irish and German

Americans who had been sympathetic to fascism, or anti–New Deal Republicans—overlook the true extent of McCarthy's support. A Gallup poll in March 1954 showed that 46 percent of the American population had "a favorable opinion" of the junior senator from Wisconsin. [10] According to his most recent scholarly biographer, Thomas C. Reeves, McCarthy remained popular among newspaper editors and radio commentators even after he had fallen from honor in the Senate and within his own party. Reeves also notes the events that overlapped McCarthy's senatorial career and help explain his political ascendancy. The Korean War between the Soviet-backed North Koreans and the American-backed South Koreans coincided with his investigation. Information had been surfacing since the late forties about Communists who had obtained sensitive government positions during the war. In 1950 the British discovered that Klaus Fuchs, an atomic physicist who had formerly worked at Los Alamos, had given atomic secrets to the Soviets. Equally important for understanding the bitter anticommunism of the early fifties were the forced Sovietization of Eastern Europe and the fall of mainland China to Communist forces in 1949. [11]

In 1954 two conservatives in their twenties, William F. Buckley, Jr., and his brother-in-law Brent Bozell, wrote a defense of McCarthy's career as a Senate investigator. Their work, *McCarthy and His Enemies,* was concerned not only with substantiating McCarthy's charges but also with discussing the moral question that they believed he had raised at least by indirection. William S. Schlamm, an Austrian émigré, asserted in the prologue that political commitments mattered for McCarthyites. Those who had served, or had apologized for, Stalin bore a continuing responsibility for once aiding the Communist enemy. Buckley and Bozell viewed the struggle between McCarthy and his liberal enemies as one between the defenders of American society and the advocates of moral anarchy: "Not only is it characteristic of society to create institutions and to defend them with sanctions. Societies must do so . . . or else they cease to exist." [12] Conservatives believed that McCarthy's enemies were their own: the moral relativists who absolutized the open society. In a postscript on the McCarthy era in 1957, the usually skeptical James Burnham observed that the "issue was philosophical, metaphysical." Burnham thought liberals were correct, from their point of view, in discrediting McCarthy, because he had challenged their "secularist, egalitarian, relativist" understanding of the world. [13]

Libertarians who helped launch the postwar conservative movement embraced the interpretation of McCarthyism implicit in Burnham's comments. A striking case in point was Frank Chodorov. The son of Russian Jewish immigrants, he had become a libertarian as a young man, under the influence of Thoreau and the late-nineteenth-century social reformer Henry George. While Chodorov campaigned for George's plan for a single tax on unproductive land, he came into contact with Albert Jay Nock, another advocate of the single tax. With Nock's support, Chodorov was made a staff member of the *Freeman,* and after thirty years of involvement with that twice-refounded periodical, became, like other disciples of Nock, part of the founding generation of postwar conservatism.

Chodorov's thinking underwent definite changes, particularly from the end of the war until his death in 1966. He himself was affected by the broad conservative movement that he had worked to create—and that ultimately carried him beyond his early individualistic creed. Despite his religious skepticism and passionate belief in individual liberty, Chodorov sought the collaboration of religious conservatives, Southern regionalists, and others of a traditionalist persuasion when he organized the Intercollegiate Society of Individualists. His earliest collaborator in this enterprise, William Buckley, held theological views radically different from his. Yet Buckley, in a particularly moving obituary, notes that Chodorov grew increasingly concerned toward the end of his life with the moral preconditions for liberty. Chodorov was among the earliest to praise *McCarthy and His Enemies* and recommended it to readers of the *Freeman* as soon as it appeared.[14]

During the McCarthy era, prominent libertarians of the Right, notably Chodorov and John Chamberlain, asked the same critical questions about civil liberties as did other conservatives. By contrast, anticommunists who were social democrats, like Sidney Hook and Melvin Lasky, reacted less dramatically to what they perceived as the evils of communism. They did protest the absence of intellectual freedom in the Soviet bloc and organized the American Committee for Cultural Freedom in 1949.[15] The committee was to publicize the attack on free inquiry that took place under dictatorial regimes. But the libertarians of the Right considered such steps to be inadequate in a struggle between the principle of individuality and the total state. They also viewed the noncommunist intellectual Left as a soft ally with the same collectivist values as those the Communists claimed to honor. James Burnham often made this observation to his readers.

Some maverick libertarians, for example, Max Eastman, who remained a crusading atheist until the end of his life, unexpectedly became McCarthyites. But other libertarians turned zealously anticommunist as part of a deeper philosophical conversion. They were responding to the kinds of arguments that Buckley and Bozell made about the limits of the open society. Libertarians were also taking another look at the American experience. Yale professor of political theory Willmoore Kendall emphasized that the postwar notions of civil liberties were thoroughly modern. In interpreting the Bill of Rights in his essays, Kendall focused on the dispute between federalists and states rightists at the time of America's founding. The Tenth Amendment, which recognized state authority under the new federal system, he held to be basic to understanding the entire Bill of Rights.[16] Kendall warned against wrenching the First Amendment's guarantee of freedom of expression from its historical context. States rightists at the constitutional convention, said Kendall, favored a Bill of Rights in order to prevent the new federal government from exercising power which they wished to have reserved to the states. Kendall found ample precedents, going back to the early republic, for laws against sedition. He also quoted the Founding Fathers to underline their differences from modern interpreters of the First Amendment.[17]

Kendall and Buckley both insisted that the exercise of liberty was predicated on historical precedents and moral restraints without which all liberty degenerated into anarchy. They justified the suspension of ordinary First Amendment rights to known Communists by going beyond the appeal to pressing circumstances. Nor did they dwell on liberal hypocrisy in their discussion of civil liberties. For example, neither Buckley nor Kendall made much of the fact that the American Civil Liberties Union had repeatedly defended the wartime expropriation and resettlement of Japanese Americans. Postwar conservatives, and even those libertarians among them, were less concerned about liberal hypocrisy than about the proper limits of intellectual freedom. Although Buckley does observe that the American intellectual Left supported the House Committee on Un-American Activities while it was being used (up to 1945) to investigate suspected Fascists, his quarrel with liberals in *McCarthy and His Enemies* was mostly unrelated to this problem of inconsistency. He criticized liberals for denying, or pretending to deny, that American society should protect its values "against competing values."[18] Kendall let it be known that he opposed Communists as a "majoritarian democrat." Because their views and practices were inimical to the American political and moral sense, as he understood it, Communists were not entitled to consideration as legitimate members of the political community.

Despite the journalistic assistance that Republican politicians received from postwar conservatives during and after the McCarthy era, their agendas did not coincide. Midwestern Senators, most notably Robert A. Taft, William Bricker, and William E. Jenner, were quick to exploit popular indignation against the Roosevelt-Truman administration that had allowed Communists and fellow travelers to work for it, but Republican isolationism remained strong into the 1950s. By contrast, the postwar conservatives, including those who founded *National Review,* advocated massive American intervention against Soviet expansion. The architects of their foreign policy—Burnham and Meyer—believed that the very survival of the West depended upon maintaining pressure on the Soviet empire. Only Western assertiveness, under the political leadership of a powerful America, would keep the Soviets from expanding their sphere of control. Burnham and other postwar conservatives like Stefan Possony and Robert Strausz-Hupé were convinced that the war against the Soviets and their clients would continue until one side or the other had won.[19] They stressed the centrality of Communist ideology in explaining the relentlessly expansionist nature of the Soviet state. Communist states did not operate in accordance with the kind of political principles that had informed traditional (including czarist) statecraft. They strove by every means to bring noncommunist societies under their control, practicing political coexistence only as a temporary expedient.

In the ideological struggle that the American intellectual Right waged against communism, it drew heavily upon former Communists and Central European émigrés. Both were disproportionately present in the conservative intellectual movement of the 1950s. Although studies have already appeared on the specifically Marxist background of some postwar conservatives, the European roots of these and other conservatives deserves further attention. Almost all the repentant Communists who became conservatives were either originally from Central Europe—like Willi Schlamm, and the cultural anthropologist Karl Wittfogel—or had come out of Central European home environments—like Will Herberg and Frank Meyer—or in the cases of Burnham and Chambers had been strongly affected by European culture and ideas. The writing and thinking of these émigrés inevitably reflected a European point of reference: for example, when they described the struggle between Marxism and Western civilization as a dialectic of historical forces; or when they treated the American experience within the broader framework of Western civilization. Like the German philosopher Hegel, these modern conservatives interpreted history as a process that revealed the interaction of competing spiritual principles.[20]

Revolt of the Masses

Another side of postwar conservatism was also affected by European thought: the traditionalist critique of American mass culture. Herbert J. Gans traces this critique in the postwar years to those who were descended "from the European elite or who modeled themselves on it." Although Gans goes too far in ascribing a European pedigree to postwar traditionalism, his perception is valuable. Postwar conservatism in its cultural manifestations reflected the values of European civilization as much as those of the American heartland. [21]

Russell Kirk is a case in point: although descended from New England Puritans and the author of a monograph on the Southern political thinker, John Randolph, Kirk still drew inspiration from Edmund Burke and Sir Walter Scott for his portrait of the "conservative mind." Kirk justified these transatlantic influences by describing the object of his study as a hyphenated entity, an "Anglo-American" mind that he first undertook to analyze as a student at St. Andrew's in Scotland. The conservative sociologist Robert Nisbet has tried to revive the study of French and German counterrevolutionaries for the light they shed on the dissolution of social bonds in the modern world. Two German émigrés—scholars who enjoyed the respect of postwar conservatives Leo Strauss and Eric Voegelin—exalted the ideals of classical antiquity, although the mystic Voegelin and the rationalist Strauss differed over the natures of the ideals they wished to return to. While Hayek, a Central European, considers himself an "old-fashioned liberal," he too betrays a European traditionalist pedigree. Hayek laments the vulgarization of political and social life under the welfare state. He admires nineteenth-century middle-class society and holds up the model of the traditional Swiss confederation as an example of a soundly functioning republic.

The Protracted Struggle of *National Review*

The "protracted struggle" against the Soviets, and the appeal to moral norms in the context of this civilizational struggle, were recurrent themes in the early issues of *National Review.* In an editorial for *National Review* on 16 January 1962, William F. Buckley, Jr., defended the House Committee on Un-American Activities in America. Stating ideas that he and other *National Review* editors presented in greater detail in a book published in 1962, Buckley pilloried absolutist civil libertarians. Resuming themes already developed in *McCarthy and His Enemies,* Buckley professed to be amazed at how far liberals carried the principles of freedom of expression and association in dealing with Marxist revolutionaries: "The superstition that the hands of truth will rout the vermin of error seems, like a fragment of Victorian lace, quaint, but too brittle to be lifted out of the showcase. . . . We need to make definite strides forward in a political theory of freedom suitable to a world in which things like Communists and atom bombs exist."[22] On 10 April 1962, Jewish theologian and *National Review* writer Will Herberg offered similar observations in reviewing his colleagues' work, *The Committee and Its Critics.* Although Herberg, too, stated his belief in freedom as a political and spiritual value, like Buckley he stressed the struggle for civilization as the necessary context for understanding constitutional rights: "It is only when 'un-American' propaganda becomes a part of a conspiratorial movement allied with a foreign enemy bent on the destruction of our nation, of freedom, and of Western civilization that it becomes a proper subject for congressional inquiry, disclosure, and legislation."[23] It should be noted that Herberg justified the Congressional investigation by appealing to a clear and present danger. Unlike Buckley and Kendall, he did not insist on making the concept of civil liberties fit a traditionalist social philosophy.

In the fifties and sixties, the editors of *National Review* saw themselves more as the custodians of the cultural past (epitomized in the phrase "Western civilization") than as the promoters of civil liberty or of democratic equality. This preference was evident in their response to the drive to create a black electorate in the South. Although Frank Meyer often invoked states' rights doctrine during the early phase of the civil-rights movement, the essential principle for him and other *National Review* conservatives was to maintain traditional Western values against an easily radicalized black voting bloc. The editors of *National Review* took this stand emphatically in a controversial statement of belief on 24 August 1957: "Should the White South be allowed to take such measures as are necessary to prevail politically and culturally, in areas where it does not predominate numerically? The shocking answer is Yes—the white community is so entitled because, for the time being, it is the advanced race. *National Review* believes that the South's premises are correct. If the majority wills what is socially atavistic, then to thwart the majority may be, though undemocratic, enlightened."[24]

National Review published articles in defense of this position by the Southern regionalist Virginius Dabney and James Jackson Kilpatrick, but by the mid-sixties some writers began to find other grounds for opposing the mounting demands of the civil-rights movement. Civil-rights activists and their supporters in Congress and among the judiciary were calling for far-reaching government efforts, such as the busing of students and the surveillance of the private sector, in order to achieve full racial integration. Dartmouth literary critic Jeffrey Hart, a later editor of *National Review,* ridiculed the attempt to "effect total Negro integration" as a "novel abstract pattern" that went counter to the process of social integration undergone by other ethnic groups in America.[25] The utopian aims of the civil-rights movement, were they to be realized, required the transformation of established cultural and social patterns. In a similar vein, Frank Meyer noted the shift from a "civil rights agitation toward confiscatory socialism."[26] Hart, Meyer, and Will Herberg all identified the civil-rights agitation of the sixties with social-engineering plans that would destroy communities that had been independent of bureaucratic control. In *Suicide of the West,* James Burnham supplemented these attacks on the revolutionary impulse of American liberals with critical observations on their "relentlessly driven" character. The liberal tries to overthrow the past because of his emotional makeup: "Even when there is no objective reason to believe that what he does can solve the problem," he presses on remorselessly "to appease the guilt in his own breast."[27]

Faith of Our Fathers

A traditionalism that invoked a vanished past was another part of post-war conservatism. Two seminal thinkers of this traditionalist revival were Richard M. Weaver (1910–63) and his more prolific admirer Russell Kirk (1918–). In his cultural criticism and essays on political rhetoric, Weaver identified himself as a Southern regionalist and an ethical Platonist.

A militant critic of moral relativism and mass culture, Weaver defended agrarian hierarchical values which he saw honored in the antebellum South and, in varying degrees, throughout Western civilization before World War I. Weaver was critical of the material and psychological reductionism that he associated with the social sciences and other characteristically modern disciplines. He believed that the failure of intellectuals to take the force of ideas seriously was one more symptom of "the dissolution of the West."[28]

As a Southern man of letters, the conservative Weaver was hardly an isolated phenomenon. A student and disciple of such prominent Southern writers as Donald Davidson and Andrew Lytle, Weaver was heir to an agrarian tradition of thought that crystallized around the 1930 manifesto *I'll Take My Stand,* a work that included contributions by John Crowe

Ransom, Allen Tate, Andrew Lytle, Robert Penn Warren, and Donald Davidson. Despite differences in their opinions, the agrarians shared a conviction, transmitted to Weaver, that a strictly commercial civilization, divorced from the land and from tradition, lacked moral and spiritual roots. Because of their literary fame, agrarian writers were able to secure a hearing for their reactionary views out of all proportion with their numbers. They also succeeded in attracting disciples. In addition to Weaver and literary critic Cleanth Brooks, writers influenced by the agrarians include literary critics M. E. Bradford, and Marion Montgomery, poets Wendell Berry, Fred Chappell, and George Garrett, and the historian essayist Clyde N. Wilson.

Russell Kirk—a "Northern agrarian" and an admirer of Weaver—exerted perhaps a more profound influence on postwar thought, largely through his book *The Conservative Mind* (1953). William Rusher considers Kirk's study together with *The Road to Serfdom* and Whittaker Chambers's *Witness* the "three most powerful contributions to the conservative movement that was stirring intellectually in the early 1950s."[29]

In *The Conservative Mind* Kirk sets out to achieve two objects, both related to the task of creating a self-confident American conservative movement. First, he attempts to prove that, contrary to those who consider progressive thinking the American mainstream, "liberal" ideas have not generally defined the American experience. Kirk traces a continuing traditionalist strain among Anglo-American authors and statesmen, from the eloquent critic of the French Revolution, Edmund Burke, to the poet and literary critic, T. S. Eliot. Although he concedes that the present age of commercial greed and innovating zeal is hostile to the conservative impulse, Kirk finds congenial thoughts in the writings of such diverse minds as Nathaniel Hawthorne, James Fenimore Cooper, John C. Calhoun, John Adams, and Henry Adams.[30]

Second, Kirk undertakes to define conservatism as a body of belief. This body of belief, he argues, has been present and sometimes dominant in the Anglo-American culture since the late eighteenth century. He sums up the cardinal tenets of true conservatives in an introductory chapter that leans heavily toward nineteenth-century British conservatism. Kirk proclaims that social hierarchy is necessary to the proper order of the world, and he affirms both historical Providence and the divine source of traditional morality. He expresses his "affection for the proliferating variety and mystery of traditional life," his "faith in prescription" and in the role of imagination as a source of morals. He defends "the persuasion that property and freedom are inseparably connected." Kirk ends his statement of conservative belief with the observation "that change and reform are not identical and that innovation is a devouring conflagration more often than it is a torch of progress."[31]

Although Kirk later denied the dogmatic intent of his "canons of conservative thought," his rigorous formulation may have given many conservatives a coherent philosophy for the first time. Unlike Weaver, Kirk and his followers had not given up on the present age. They sought to restore America and the Western world to what they thought were its first principles. The postwar traditionalists found these postulates, not in the Age of Reason which Thomas Paine celebrated, but in a civilization extending back through the medieval schoolmen to classical and biblical antiquity. Rusher (among others) enthusiastically praises Kirk's "traditionalist heritage of Burkean conservatism."[32] But Kirk in fact expounded more than one "Burkean conservatism." The Burke of *The Conservative Mind* was a critic of political rationalism, a traditionalist who appealed to "prejudice and prescription," inbred sentiments, and inherited rights, as the basis of political order. Kirk repeated Burke's warnings about viewing civil society as something artificial, a dissoluble agreement made to further individual self-interest. He was especially fond of Burke's description of the true social contract that bound together all generations—and the higher and lower natures of man.

In the late fifties, Kirk also found in Burke's writings a natural law doctrine that the Catholic scholars Peter Stanlis and Francis Canavan had first discovered there.[33] Catholic conservative interest in Burke (who came from an Irish Catholic family and was a lifelong supporter of Catholic emancipation in England) went back in America to the forties. On 12 April 1945, the Burke Society was founded at Fordham University to foster a return to "the principles, values, and truths which are the heritage of the political and international society of Christendom." Kirk's later interpretation of Burke echo these sentiments, stressing Burke's ties to medieval and classical conceptions of the "higher law." According to this second view, Burke criticized revolution and abstract schemes being applied to political life, above all, as a member of Christendom, of a civilization that contained moral norms within its evolving historical institutions.[34]

Kirk found other sources for his conservative philosophy, both more recent and closer to home, in the writings of two Harvard alumni, Irving Babbitt and Paul Elmer More. As a scholar, Babbitt was well-known for his studies of Sanskrit literature and for his interpretations of nineteenth-century French literature. More was a Neoplatonist who became famous as a result of his literary and philosophical essays. Between Babbitt's secularized Buddhism, with its ethic of moral restraint and hard work, and More's attachment to Platonic ethics, a school of thought emerged that came to be known as the New Humanism. Despite the tirades of H. L. Mencken and Sinclair Lewis (in his 1930 Nobel Prize acceptance speech, Lewis referred to "a doctrine of the blackest reaction introduced into a stirringly revolutionary world"), the New Humanism won many learned adherents in the late 1920s and early thirties; and well into the postwar years, young professors of literature were deriving inspiration from the ethical insights of Babbitt and More. Among the better-known literary and cultural critics influenced by the New Humanism have been T. S. Eliot, Peter Viereck, Austin Warren, George Panichas, the neo-Hegelian Claes Ryn, and—of course—Kirk himself.

The traditionalist ideas of the postwar conservative movement were essential to the process of conservative self-definition. The traditionalists gave to the American Right a set of interlocking beliefs that addressed religious and moral concerns. They appealed to the historical conscious-ness of a civilization that went back beyond the American past, into the medieval and ancient worlds. And though not reducible to any particular economic system, traditionalist beliefs were seen as compatible with a capitalist economy. Outside the South (where conservative intellectuals were often hostile to commerce), traditionalists made common cause with libertarians, while professing, like William Buckley, a higher alle-giance to theological than economic matters. A distaste for social engi-neering united the two sides. In his six "canons of conservative thought," Kirk affirms that private property is a moral and social good. "Radical systems," says Kirk, attack established property relations in order to destroy family and communal ties. Precisely for that reason, Kirk and other traditionalists supported private enterprise against what they be-lieved was an egalitarian welfare state.

Traditionalists and libertarians could also agree on common heroes. The libertarian idol Jefferson (whom Albert Jay Nock celebrated in a pop-ular biography) was also the figure whom Southern conservatives exalted as an agrarian and states rightist. Albert Jay Nock, a cultural elitist, had fans among traditionalists and libertarians; both groups mourned his passing in 1945. Through the autobiographical *Memoirs of a Superfluous Man,* Nock left his mark on two later traditionalist thinkers, Russell Kirk and Robert Nisbet, both American soldiers when they first read his book. Each claimed that his life was profoundly changed by this man who con-demned the modern state as "our enemy."[35] Both brought forth their most powerful indictments of modern social fragmentation in the same year, 1953, when Kirk published *The Conservative Mind* and Nisbet *The Quest for Community.*

Traditionalists and libertarians felt equally comfortable with certain economists whom both chose to honor. One was Wilhelm Roepke, an émigré from Nazi Germany who had gone to teach in Geneva and who vigorously defended both free enterprise and social custom. Roepke attacked socialist economies as much for their radicalizing effect on society as their incompatibility with individual freedom and initiative. Hayek also appealed to conservative as well as libertarian readers. In his postwar writings, the famous Austrian economist showed increasing appreciation for the evolutionary and organic view of society that he discovered in the writing of Burke. Hayek's concern with individual self-development in *The Road to Serfdom* was balanced in his later work by an increasing emphasis on the cultural and moral foundations of a free society. The widespread conservative interest in Burke went still further in bridging the distance between traditionalists and libertarians. Burke had claimed to despise revolutions but had supported American colonial grievances in the 1770s. Though a social traditionalist, he had praised the free market and had frequently cited Adam Smith's critique of mercantilism from *Wealth of Nations.*[36]

Buckley, Kendall, Chodorov, and others on the Right appealed to moral and metaphysical values as the necessary foundation of a free society. By the mid-fifties libertarians and traditionalists were embracing a synthesis of ideas that included absolute truths and personal liberty. The figure who tried hardest to build a theoretical bridge between the two was the Christian libertarian Frank Meyer. Meyer believed that his two overriding principles, freedom and moral-social authority, had already been synthesized in the founding documents of the American regime. The Founding Fathers had brought together traditions that had remained "bifurcated" in European politics: "The emphasis of virtue and value and order and the emphasis on freedom and the integrity of the individual."[37] Meyer himself justified liberty as an instrumental good and insisted that his position was in line with the authentic American political tradition of "fusionism." America's founders knew that political and personal freedoms were only beneficial for those who lived as loyal members of a community. By the same token, they recognized that only a free society allowed men to *choose* virtue, to will what is moral instead of having it imposed.

Meyer found the welfare state incompatible with both freedom and virtue. The modern "leviathan" state that Meyer despised was a product of the French Revolution's attempt to reconstruct human nature. Since the end of the eighteenth century, starting with the Age of Reason (from which Meyer always dissociated the shaping principles of the American regime), rationalists had been devising utopian schemes. In Europe these rash innovators had worked through revolution, but in America, bureaucrats and social engineers had managed to produce far-reaching social changes without political violence. The results, Meyer maintained, were similar in both cases: established patterns of community and long-accepted moral authority were sacrificed to the god of progress. Meyer believed that the activist Supreme Court under Earl Warren exemplified this tendency. An unelected body vastly exceeding the authority that the Founding Fathers had assigned to it, the Supreme Court, as viewed by Meyer, was enacting its own vision of an integrated, secularized humanity without being accountable to any power beyond itself. The Court had no more regard for the Constitution than for the American public. It gave that document increasingly broad meanings, selectively looking for constitutional phrases that could be adapted to its reforming mission.[38]

Although Meyer thought that his historical theory would produce agreement on policy as well as principle, events proved him wrong. Some of his disciples, for example, went beyond him as advocates of individual liberty. Some emphatically rejected his views on Negro civil rights, maintaining that he had allowed his cultural prejudices to warp his judgment of the racial situation. David Brudnoy, one of his long-time disciples, expressed support for feminism and for movements aiming at black cultural self-expression. Meyer's more traditionalist admirers found him indecisive when it came to strong laws against pornography. Critics on the Right tried to elicit his libertarian opinions on censorship in the presence of young conservatives. Such a tactic, it was hoped, would lead more traditionally minded students into second thoughts about the "free-thinking Meyer"—or, better still, force Meyer into rethinking his own views.

Despite these battles, Meyer's fusionist view fitted the developing conservative vision of his time. It bestowed on that vision theoretical unity and the benefits of an extensive reading of the American and more general Western past. Although Meyer picked quarrels with traditionalists (particularly Russell Kirk) and with extreme libertarians (such as Max Eastman) and with the usually impassive James Burnham (whom he found insufficiently patriotic), he did so from the vital center of the conservative culture of the 1950s. More than anyone else, he constructed the edifice of ideas that would accommodate various conservative positions. And he achieved this not through a jerry-built structure of thought, but by carefully studying the past—albeit from his own perspective. He focused on the moral intention of America's founders and the cultural-religious traditions that had nurtured the American people. Meyer believed that most Americans inwardly accepted the fusion of positions that defined conservatism as a political force: economic libertarianism, cultural traditionalism, local government, and militant anticommunism. He insisted, until his death in 1972, that a conservative political majority would rear itself up as soon as Americans discovered what had happened to their constitutional and moral legacy.

Other conservatives accepted his fusionist view at least operationally. This is dramatically apparent from a debate that took place in *National Review* on 30 January 1962 between several members of its staff and M. Morton Auerbach, a prominent critic of postwar conservatism. Auerbach mocked the conservative world view of the journal as a "fallacious attempt to link medievalism with classical liberalism," an error that Auerbach stated was already present in Edmund Burke.[39] The staff responded with a defense of the conservative case for ordered liberty. M. Stanton Evans, the future founder of the American Conservative Union, observed that what Auerbach called "inconsistency" was "in fact the vital equilibrium centered in the wisdom of conservatism, of the free society." Kirk, the traditionalist, maintained that the opposition to "the contemporary aggrandizement of the state" was founded on respect for "the freedom of the person." Such respect was quintessentially medieval and Christian since it presupposed human spirituality and denied power to a totalist, secular state. Meyer affirmed also that American conservatism was being consistent in fighting simultaneously for personal-material freedoms and traditional religious values: "American conservatives do not want to return to medieval conditions. They do wish, in modern conditions, to preserve and develop the tension between the transcendent ends of man and the freedom through which he can attain those ends, the tension which Western civilization has always expressed."

A fusionist view of the conservative tradition that incorporated freedom and moral-religious authority provided a common ground for Auerbach's respondents. *National Review* and *Modern Age* (a traditionalist journal founded by Kirk in 1957) may have gone too far in treating the pieces of what became the dominant conservative view as a seamless and self-evident whole. Yet, the pieces did fit together well enough to allow self-labeled conservatives who read conservative journals to agree on a common identity.

Auerbach, however, may have scored one point against his opponents on the Right. Fusionism, once triumphant among conservatives (even implicitly among Meyer's traditionalist critics), engendered political and intellectual problems that were not yet fully apparent in 1962. The mechanical yoking of religious and cultural traditionalism, free market teachings, and an activist foreign policy would result in making conservative principles appear politically partisan and inescapably modernist. T. S. Eliot foresaw this development in his correspondence with Russell Kirk. On 13 January 1956, the poet—a defender of royalism and Anglo-Catholicism—wrote in response to Kirk's request for his opinion about *National Review*: "It seems to me too consciously the vehicle of a defiant minority."[40] A true conservative journal, said Eliot, would "put a good deal of emphasis on ideas and principles." In a subsequent letter to Kirk, Eliot objected to the editorial decision by *National Review* to have Joseph McCarthy (more likely a ghost writer) review the memoirs of Dean Acheson, whom McCarthy had repeatedly ridiculed in his speeches: "Such an article would carry more weight with a reader like myself if written by almost anyone else."[41]

Meyer epitomized the activist spirit on the postwar Right. Comparing conservatives to the church militant (and calling his column in *National Review* "Doctrines and Heresies"), he exhorted his readers to bring America back from the edge of catastrophe. In one particularly spirited column for *National Review,* he aimed his shafts at those who taught that the welfare state would grow smaller without the capital to pay for its programs. Such a view, Meyer, stated, made no allowance for the habits of servility that socialism instilled. The American people would rid themselves of "welfarism" only by recognizing its inhumanity: "the levelling that by reducing man to a statistical number degrades all men. . . ." Conservatives were urged to go before the public and to rally "men of spirit."[42]

The problem with such rhetoric is that it tied together all policy decisions with the overriding moral goals of "saving the Republic" and Western civilization. Proceeding from his fusionist understanding of politics, Meyer attached cosmic implications to every issue that he wrote on. Fiscal questions were raised to philosophic-existential issues as part of a struggle for the soul of mankind. The good side, as much as the bad, in this struggle held views that were seen as being of a piece. Meyer viewed his own fusionism as a true wedding of liberty and moral order. Any calm reflection on "politics' principles, or lack of principles" of the kind that Eliot recommended, went against Meyer's very nature.

In the late 1960s Meyer wrote against George Wallace's attempt to run a presidential campaign based on economic programs and opposition to liberal social policies. Although Meyer favored a populist revolt against social engineering, he considered Wallace an inappropriate leader for such a movement. He denounced Wallace, together with main-line Democrats, as unsuited to govern America and as "alien to the American conservative conception of constitutional republican government."[43] In 1968 Meyer took the view that all philosophically and politically sound conservatives were, like him, supporting the presidential bid of Richard M. Nixon. Noting the "civilizational crisis of 1968" unleashed by urban riot, he maintained that "Nixon's administration will turn the tide of the anarchy that threatens to engulf us."[44] The expressions "civilizational content" and "civilizational consensus" invariably accompanied Meyer's statements of political preference.

The appeal to activism became an integral part of postwar conservatism. Almost all of *National Review*'s staff participated in political campaigns: for example, Frank Meyer as vice-chairman of the New York Conservative party; William Rusher as an advisor to Barry Goldwater; and William Buckley as a candidate for mayor of New York City in 1965. This activist enthusiasm even spread into the ranks of traditionalists. A repugnance for modern political life had been characteristic of the early Richard Weaver. Although Weaver did write for *National Review, Modern Age,* and the publications of the Intercollegiate Society of Individualists, he felt little hope for the modern world of mass democracy and the cult of technology. In one (now famous) elegiac passage from the foreword to his book *Ideas Have Consequences,* Weaver offers this lament: "It seems to me that the world is now more than ever dominated by the gods of mass and speed and that the worship of these can lead only to the lowering of standards, the adulteration of quality, and, in general, to the loss of these things which are essential to the life of civility and culture."[45] The author of these lines (written in 1947) would ten years later be participating in citizens' councils in order to resist the forced introduction of racial integration into Southern schools. Another Southern conservative and antimodernist, Donald Davidson, the scholar and poet, took a similar position in the fifties. Like Weaver, his old student, Davidson opposed what he considered the equalizing, bureaucratic state through a gesture that he believed would have no real political significance. Davidson poignantly described his own plight, as a poet and "out-right traditionalist," predicting "the ruin of modern, secularized society," while being "unheard or unheeded." All that he had was "the poet's curse," which he invoked "upon the deaf ears and faceless bodies" around him.[46]

Although expressions of futility can also be found in *The Conservative Mind,* Kirk became more involved in politics than either Weaver or Davidson, whether as a delegate to Republican state conventions in Michigan or as a supporter of Barry Goldwater. Others on Kirk's side went well beyond him in pursuing political agendas. In 1962 traditionalist intellectuals set up the New York Conservative party, a group founded in accordance with their ideology. By the 1960s postwar conservatism had become a political movement that tried to appeal to members of both national parties, by defending economic liberty and traditional social values and by opposing the expansion of Soviet communism. The activist phase that conservatism entered by the 1960s changed it significantly—and sometimes in ways that offended the theorists of the forties and fifties. This activism, however, was already implicit in the world view of the *Freeman* and in articles printed in *National Review* and *Modern Age.* Although the first generation of postwar conservatism found much to deplore about the present time, they believed things could be set right. They themselves took the initiative when they moved from theory into practice.

Chapter Two

Before and after Goldwater: Conservatism in the Sixties

The conservative movement of the 1960s was held together more by ideological concerns than by economic interests. It is true that conservatives did appeal to opponents of an expanding welfare system by demanding harder eligibility tests for welfare recipients; they also advocated economic deregulation and spoke nostalgically of an older capitalist America. Despite such rhetoric, bankers and industrialists, outside of areas in the South and Southwest, withheld their support from candidates with "conservative party" labels.[1] In 1964 their preferred Republican presidential candidate was not the conservative Barry Goldwater but the more liberal Nelson Rockefeller.[2] Big business feared the election of visionary conservatives who might have threatened its working relations with government agencies. Though conservatives called for lightening the tax burden related to welfare, their programs, as many discovered, had another side. Their political candidates made no secret of their commitment to a strong military and to a more vigorous struggle against Soviet power.

Like the Socialists and Catholics in the German Empire between 1871 and 1918 whose party affiliations signified the acceptance of a worldview, the American conservatives of the 1960s based politics on a shared moral universe. They thought that elected office was a means for attaining ideological goals, not one for furthering material interests. In this respect, conservatives foreshadowed their Leftist counterparts of the late sixties, who also came largely from the professional and leisure classes. Both groups disavowed the interest politics James Madison had once viewed as natural, and even beneficent, for the American regime; each preferred to offer the American people a politics of ideas. Moreover, Right and Left in the 1960s turned for principles and programs to engaged intellectuals grouped around journals and universities.

The Campus Right

Seymour Martin Lipset helped to formulate the standard opinion in a study of student politics in the 1960s, when he associated Right-wing student activism predominantly with small church-affiliated colleges. This assumption was based on reliable data found in an investigation by Richard G. Braungart of student activism in the sixties. The largest conservative campus organization (founded in 1961), Young Americans for Freedom, drew fewer members from state universities and prestige institutions of higher learning than did its far-Left counterpart, Students for a Democratic Society. Unlike SDS, YAF was heavily represented in sectarian colleges and among students who professed religious allegiances. Lipset and Braungart also point out that YAF members generally were poorer and more vocationally oriented than student activists on the Left.[3]

Whatever its other merits, such information does not explain the origins of a conservative political movement on American campuses. Such a development began in large, widely respected universities, among faculty and students with a deeply theoretical bent. For example, the University of Chicago played a formative role in creating a conservative movement as well as a conservative world view. The economics department contained outstanding defenders of capitalism such as Friedman, Knight, and George Stigler. Richard Weaver taught English and rhetoric in the University College; Friedrich von Hayek lectured on social philosophy to both undergraduates and graduate students; and another Central European émigré at Chicago, who occupied an endowed chair in political thought, Leo Strauss, attacked "value-relativity" as the mortal sin of the American intelligentsia. Friedman, Hayek, and Strauss all underlined the importance of putting sound teachings into political practice, and their students went into government as well as academic careers.

By the late fifties, Yale University was becoming another training ground for conservative activists. In the late forties, Willmoore Kendall had taught political philosophy there to the young William Buckley, just returned from military service. Though Buckley, in his first published book, *God and Man at Yale* (1952), protested the pervasive liberalism of the Yale professoriate, he nonetheless had kind words for Kendall. At Yale Buckley and his future brother-in-law Brent Bozell set about organizing the Conservative party in the Political Union. What began primarily as a discussion group of politically like-minded students that debated other such groups became a vehicle for preparing future conservative activists.[4] The same was even more true for the Party of the Right, an offshoot of Yale's Conservative party. Out of the Party of the Right came new contributors to *National Review* and eventually New Right activists of the seventies and eighties such as Anthony Dolan, Ron Docksai, and Larry Uzzell.[5]

In the 1960s Catholic universities, such as Fordham and St. John's in New York and Notre Dame, were especially important as centers of conservative activity. Fordham and St. John's provided support for both the postwar Burke revival and the organization of the New York Conservative party. Notre Dame was the focal point of a Catholic-conservative synthesis of thought to which publications such as the *Natural Law Forum,* the *Review of Politics,* and, later, the *New Scholasticism* were intended to contribute. Behind these journals stood committed Catholics or Anglo-Catholics who complained of the moral decline of the West. They saw Communist expansion as the nemesis of the West's spiritual decreptitude and of the lack of political will among its leaders. Waldemar Gurian, Stephen Kertesz, the Reverend Stanley Parry, and Gerhard Niemeyer, all political science professors, and Clarence Manion and Charles Rice of the law school represented these conservative tendencies among the Notre Dame faculty. The same tendencies could be found at the University of Dallas, which in the 1970s became a self-declared citadel of Catholic and traditional values. There Willmoore Kendall went to teach (and was converted to Catholicism) after years of social isolation at Yale. Disciples of Leo Strauss and of Richard Weaver graced the faculty at Dallas; the political science department boasted not only Kendall but Frederick Wilhelmsen, a conservative Catholic critic of secular democracy and one of the more provocative contributors to *National Review.* The University of Dallas also had one of the largest and most influential chapters of Young Americans for Freedom.

This brings us to a critical link between the early history of the conservative political movement, including its student phase, and the Catholic affiliation of many of its members. Of YAFers polled in the midsixties, 69 percent turned out to be Protestant, 26 percent Catholic, and only 5 percent Jewish. Among Leftist student activists whom the sociologist Richard Flacks interviewed in 1967, 60 percent had Jewish fathers, 36 percent were Protestant, and only 4 percent were Catholic.[6] Although social position may be one possible key to grasping the correlation between religious background and political affiliation (most Jewish Left-wing activists came from wealthier, better educated families than their Christian conservative counterparts), one should not exaggerate the rôle of this particular variable. The members of the Harvard Conservative Club and of the Yale Party of the Right were by no means socially inferior to the SDSers at Wisconsin or Michigan. Moreover, one sixth of the Jewish student activists whom the sociologist Samuel Lubell studied came from recognizable Old Left families, mostly of Eastern European origin.[7] The conservative students polled in another extensive study were mostly self-identifying members of churches, and, unlike SDS members, "felt a close relationship with one or both of their parents." The attitudes of these students cannot be entirely explained by looking to the professional or material standing of their parents.[8]

The Catholic Right

The Catholic presence in the conservative student movement was not only proportionately larger than the Protestant one but also more vital for that movement's growth. The association of conservative students with small, mostly Protestant colleges may come from identifying too closely Right-wing campus activism with a predominant type of rank-and-file member. In the early sixties, the Intercollegiate Society of Individualists introduced conservative clubs on college campuses across the country. M. Stanton Evans has described the efforts of regional directors of ISI, most conspicuously Don Lipsett in Indianapolis, to carry its literature and ideas across the American heartland.[9] Small, sectarian colleges responded favorably to this attention. Conservative clubs were formed there that placed themselves on ISI mailing lists and often voted to join YAF. But these hastily won recruits were mostly passive and typified what S. M. Lipset thought was characteristic of conservative student organizations generally: "They have not been notably successful in building a movement which has much commitment from its membership, nor have they made any real impact on the campus."[10]

In fact, the most significant form of conservative student activism did not aim at converting large state universities. Conservative students went into government and journalism and campaigned for conservative political candidates. In all these activities, Catholic students, many from Catholic colleges, made disproportionately large contributions. The post-war Right awaited them with open arms. *National Review* was accused by its critics of being militantly Catholic, a charge bitterly raised by Max Eastman before he resigned from its board. Even the Jewish editors, Meyer and Schlamm, were sympathetic to Catholic doctrine: Meyer became a Catholic on his deathbed; and Schlamm requested that a priest officiate at his funeral. The journal published the Catholic monarchists Otto von Habsburg and Erik von Kuehnelt-Leddihn; it also featured both Catholic traditionalists who were critical of the American democratic experiment, such as Wilhelmsen, Bozell, and Thomas Molnar, and such Catholic defenders of the American regime as Clare Boothe Luce and members of the Buckley family.

Unlike the vestigial secularist connection of Jewish Leftists to things Jewish, Catholic conservatives wore their religious identity as a badge of honor. Non-Catholic conservatives praised the church as an upholder of moral absolutes and, more generally, of Western civilization. The Jewish religious commentator for *National Review*, Will Herberg, even attacked the efforts at "modernizing" church rituals under Pope John XXIII. According to Herberg, Catholics who welcomed change in their ancient ceremonies were like Esau, selling their spiritual birthright for a pot of lentils.

The philocatholic attributes of the intellectual Right were related to the largely justified image of the postwar church as anticommunist and antisecularist. Catholicism may also have seemed more congruent with the emerging conservative movement than were most Protestant denominations. Throughout the twentieth century, the leadership of main-line Protestant churches had drifted to the Left, theologically and politically. The more traditional American Protestants—such as Southern Baptists and Missouri Synod Lutherans—were widely perceived as rigidly biblicist and culturally narrow. Such groups often held isolationist views of foreign policy that jarred with the anticommunist activism of the postwar Right.

Conservative political strategists became convinced that Catholics were especially receptive to their positions. Several factors contributed to that perception. The Catholic hierarchy in America and in Europe were generally outspoken anticommunists; this situation was related to, among other things, the persecution of Catholics, particularly Catholic clergymen, under the Soviet controlled states of Eastern Europe. American Catholics were also more outwardly religious than their fellow citizens.[11]

According to Gallup polls in the fifties and sixties, the percentage of Catholics who regularly attended religious services was over twice as high as the percentage for Protestants and over three times as high as the one for Jews.[12] Polling on the abortion question started in 1963 (during the furor over deformed babies whose mothers had taken thalidomide drugs); it revealed far greater Catholic than Protestant opposition to the use of abortion, even in extreme circumstances.[13]

More importantly, the backlash against liberal social policies erupted first, outside the South, in Catholic ethnic neighborhoods. In 1961 Irish Americans supported Louise Day Hicks, a Democrat opposed to forced busing, as chairman of the Boston School Board. In 1964 Irish and other Catholic voters in Massachusetts enthusiastically backed George Wallace, the former segregationist governor of Alabama, during his first foray into the North in the Democratic presidential primaries. Racial tensions, court-ordered busing, and a dramatic leap in the number of violent crimes in the 1960s made the traditionally Democratic Catholic communities in Northern cities appear to be at the point of moving permanently to the Right.

New York Conservative Party

The first group that tried to arrange a match between the postwar conservative world view and a preponderantly Catholic constituency was the New York Conservative party. The Party's "Declaration of Principles," in February 1962, opened with a statement that combined libertarian and anticommunist themes: "Our country is strong, and everywhere it is in retreat before Soviet Communism. It was founded and grew great on the free energy of free men and everywhere encroaching bureaucracy overpowers and strangles the free energy of free men." The declaration also deplored "so-called liberalism" that rendered national leaders less able "to resist the onrush of Communist conquest or to stem the subtle tide of bureaucratic socialism." To resist the foreign enemy and domestic evils, the declaration called for the reestablishment of the conservative principles of liberty, justice, and national vigilance and the vigorous pursuit of a program consonant with these principles.[14]

The Conservative party featured among its founders prominent Catholic traditionalists such as Daniel Mahoney, Henry Paolucci, and Thomas Molnar. Another cofounder, Frank Meyer, was sympathetic to the Catholic Right. Essential to the declaration is its appeal to voters as churched members of family units. The Conservative party's founders were appealing to social and moral concerns as well as pocketbook issues. Not individuals but "the fabric of society was threatened by the mounting wave of crime." The Conservative party of New York was not simply a taxpayers' league that used anticommunist rhetoric to widen its appeal. It opposed the welfare system for, among other things, the same reason it protested crime on the streets: as a symptom and cause of social degeneracy. In attacking Aid to Dependent Children, for example, the declaration criticized not the awarding of the grant but the fact that it entailed no social responsibility on the part of its recipient. The welfare mother was free to spend the money as she pleased, without being forced to use the grant on the child rather than herself. The declaration urged not that the granting of such aid be stopped but that it take place in the form of food and other necessities given directly to the child. Moreover, the same document states that if the welfare mother lives in "blatant immorality," then the state should remove the child from her care and place it (if possible) with more suitable parents.

Such proposals indicate that the New York Conservative party never viewed itself as being strictly libertarian in dealing with domestic matters. A sense of man's corporate nature—and of the power of original sin—informed the Declaration of Principles. The declaration took stands on First Amendment issues that had particularly strong appeal among Catholic voters: in favor of aid to parochial schools and in opposition to pornography. Its support of "religious observance in our public life" may also have been intended to attract the same voters; Catholics in the fifties and sixties, in responding to surveys, were far more supportive than Protestants of a religious influence being brought to bear on society. Although most of the votes involved were middle-class Republican rather than blue-collar Democratic, 25 to 30 percent of the ballots in Catholic Assembly districts in New York City went to William F. Buckley, the Conservative party's candidate for mayor, in 1965. In 1967 the Party received 71,477 votes statewide, of which 33,747 came from New York City. These votes were predominantly from non-Hispanic Catholics in Brooklyn and Queens registering concern over welfare programs and crime in their neighborhoods.[15]

Republican Majority

Despite this attempt to build an urban conservative constituency upon a Catholic ethnic base, such a strategy played no appreciable role in the conservatives' quest for the presidency in the early sixties. In 1961 conservative Republican activists, led by F. Clifton White and William Rusher, formed a committee to work for the election of a conservative president. From the start, their choices were exceedingly limited. White, Rusher, and their group—who by the end of 1961 were head-quartered in the Clarion Building, suite 3505, in midtown Manhattan—sought an electable candidate who was both an uncompromising critic of the welfare state and an anticommunist interventionist. Senator William Knowland of California was a prominent conservative who fit this de-scription. But in 1958 Knowland abandoned his Senate seat (for nonpo-litical reasons) to seek the governorship of California—which he failed to gain. In 1960 a conservative academician, John Tower, won a Senate seat from Texas. Although conservatives considered Tower insufficiently prominent to be a plausible presidential candidate, they took his election as a sign of their growing strength in the Southwest.[16]

An essay by William Rusher published in *National Review* on 12 Feb-ruary 1963 lent credibility to such thinking. Rusher maintained that con-servative Republicans could capture the presidency by winning the demographically expanding South and West, even without the Northeast and Upper Midwest.[17] Rusher, and others who were swayed by him, stressed two factors: a growing Republican vote in the once Democratic South as the national Democratic party moved to the Left and embraced unreservedly the civil rights movement; and the shift of population from the more liberal North and East into the more conservative South and West. Rusher's arguments, in some ways, anticipated those of Kevin Phillips, who in *The Emerging Republican Majority* (1969) plotted a Re-publican strategy centered on the Sunbelt and the West.

But the difference between Phillips's views and Rusher's apparent an-ticipation of them may be as significant as their oft-noted similarity. Un-like Rusher, Phillips urged Republicans and conservatives to campaign vigorously in Northern cities as well as in the South and West. A North-ern Irish Catholic and a former conservative student activist, Phillips viewed the ethnic Catholics in Northern cities and suburbs as prospective converts to the political Right. He proposed a new political coalition that would include both Sunbelt Republican and Democratic ethnics. The ar-chitects of this coalition would appeal to traditional family values and hos-tility to the counterculture and its allies in government. Phillips's model politicians would abandon anti–New Deal rhetoric and uphold the welfare state, as the price of maintaining close ties with blue-collar workers. Phillips addressed his prescription to the Republican party, which he urged to move economically to the Left and socially to the Right. He offered such advice with the benefit of hindsight, when the miscalculations of the conservative politics of the mid-sixties could already be assessed.[18]

Goldwater and After

In April 1963, White, Rusher, and their financial backers, who came predominantly from the Sunbelt, chose a Senator from Arizona, Barry Goldwater, as their presidential candidate. The group thereupon transformed itself into the Draft Goldwater Committee. According to White, Rusher, and William F. Buckley (then a nonaffiliated member of the committee), Goldwater tried long and vehemently to dissociate himself from his backers. He never believed that he could win the presidency, especially after John F. Kennedy's assassination in November 1963. Later, his presidential campaign became mired in divisive quarrels with the liberal wing of his party led by Governor Nelson Rockefeller of New York. Having emerged from party primaries with an extremist label, Goldwater spent the fall of 1964 desperately responding to the same charges from his Democratic opponent that the Rockefeller forces had leveled against him during the spring. His dissent from the 1964 Civil Rights Act—on the ground that its public-accommodations provision infringed on property rights—was construed as crass support for racism, although Goldwater had long attacked antiblack discrimination. His critical remarks during a campaign speech about public ownership of the Tennessee Valley Authority allowed him to be depicted as a reckless, indiscriminate opponent of New Deal programs. His insistence that the American government prosecute the war in Vietnam more vigorously (or leave) became for his political and journalistic adversaries proof of his belligerence.[19]

Surveying Goldwater's presidential bid, which culminated in his losing to Johnson by a margin of nearly 16 million votes and being beaten in all but six states (five in the Deep South), White observes: "It was not Republicanism that was beaten so badly in 1964, nor even the real Barry Goldwater. It was radicalism; or rather the illusion of radicalism as represented by a cruel caricature of the candidate."[20] Although White blames the Goldwater defeat partly on the effectively vicious tactics of the Johnson campaign, he also recognizes the role of historical forces. Republican opponents of the welfare state were too open in their contempt for Great Society programs: "What many of them failed to take into account was that in the latter half of the twentieth century practically everyone

wanted, indeed *expected,* something from the government and large numbers of them were perfectly willing to trade their votes in order to get
what they wanted."[21] Seen from this perspective, "Lyndon Johnson was
a conservative defending the established order, while Barry Goldwater,
the true conservative, became a 'radical' bent on upsetting the applecart
of peace and plenty." Apart from using the phrase "true conservative" to
apply to Goldwater, White's analysis foreshadows the view held by neoconservatives of the seventies and eighties looking back at the contest
of 1964.

William Rusher may have been right in calling 1964 the "watershed
year" in postwar conservatism. Goldwater was personally unable to represent the full range of postwar conservative thinking; nor was the historical moment propitious for anyone to do so. His campaign was
narrowly focused on a few economic and foreign-policy issues and on
invidious questions that journalists and politicians raised about his moral
and intellectual competence. Even if one allows for the vulgarizing process that turns philosophic principles into electoral issues, the intellectual
richness of the postwar Right, typified by James Burnham, Frank S.
Meyer, Friedrich Hayek, and Russell Kirk, was notably missing from the
Goldwater campaign. As one traditionalist critic, Craig Schiller, observed, Goldwater went down to defeat as the brutally wronged but inept
candidate of the "Hoover-Taft" wing of his party. The charge is just, even
if Schiller is inaccurate about Hoover and Taft.[22] Although Goldwater
characterized Russell Kirk as his favorite philosopher and was in turn
praised by Kirk for his anticommunist foreign policy, Goldwater could
never shake his image as a brash defender of unqualified capitalism.
Kevin Phillips criticized Goldwater and his campaign managers for paying
insufficient attention to the Northern cities, particularly their (non-
Hispanic) Catholic voters. Despite the rightward lurch of Northern ethnics in the Democratic primaries of 1964, according to Phillips, "when
November's votes were counted, the backlash was exceedingly weak.
Boston and Baltimore wards that had gone heavily for Louise Day Hicks
and George Wallace went six- and eight-to-one against Barry Goldwater."[23] Phillips correctly inferred that "[w]hatever the appeal of the 1964
GOP nominee's civil rights stance, it was outweighed by the unpopularity
of his position on labor legislation, aspects of the Social Security system
and economic issues in general (none of which handicapped free-spending
populist Democrats like Mrs. Hicks and Governor Wallace)."

After 1964 no "conservative" politician would speak as explicitly as
Goldwater had about rescinding the New Deal. Republicans would de-

nounce further deficit spending, extol individual self-reliance, and call for trimming budgets. "Conservative" politicians would repeatedly seek votes by deploring the growth of bureaucracy. Yet, the obvious lesson of 1964 would not be forgotten. The majority of the American electorate voted for the welfare state and against its unabashed critic. This electoral fact accorded with the findings of Gallup and other polls in 1964, that most Americans favored the continuation of existing federal social programs and supported the Civil Rights Act of that year. A Gallup poll of rank-and-file Republicans on 13 January 1965 revealed that their top priorities were to replace Goldwaterites, such as Dean Burch and Richard Kleindienst, in positions of party leadership and to adopt a "more moderate" platform. [24] These opinions are noteworthy even if one takes into account the bitter aftertaste of the 1964 election.

Conservative writers, particularly William Rusher and Jeffrey Hart, have tried to show the Goldwater campaign was subsequently vindicated. It produced an expanding core of Rightist activists whose principles triumphed in Ronald Reagan's election in 1980. [25] This interpretation is only half true. The 1964 presidential race created a wave of conservative political activism that continued to grow and shows no signs of receding. Coextensively with this, conservative foundations that dealt with policy questions and electoral strategies were launched. Yet, two characteristics of what has been termed "second-generation, postwar conservatism" were its lack of a philosophic (and certainly traditionalist) focus and its willingness to compromise (without admitting it) with a leftward-drifting public opinion. The traditionalist aspect of the conservative movement— represented by Kirk's Burkean defense of organic authority or Weaver's agrarian anticommercial values—had become politically irrelevant by 1964. In the 1970s even Goldwaterism became politically passé. Goldwater's *The Conscience of a Conservative* (1960), which was avidly distributed by his backers in 1964, was mostly a statement of its author's positions on leading political issues: states' rights, welfare, closed shops imposed by organized labor, and the "Soviet menace." Though Goldwater properly accused the Left of being fixated "on the material side of man's nature," it is unclear whether his own declaration of belief differed in this respect. For example, he insisted that the American educational system be limited to the "training of the mind," through the transmission of factual knowledge without moral or philosophical values. [26] His stated conviction that the formation of values take place exclusively in the family and in churches was not the purely defensive reaction to growing liberal control of education which many of Goldwater's traditionalist supporters imagined it to be. It betokened the secularist, technocratic cast of his thinking that became more pronounced in the seventies and eighties, particularly in his bitter comments against the advocates of school prayers. Goldwater by the seventies also came to advocate environmentalist restrictions. He shocked his old backers even more by defending the Supreme Court's imposition of judicial remedies to fight the effects of antiblack discrimination.[27]

Goldwaterism in its pristine form may have vanished with the challenge that Congressman John Ashbrook of Ohio mounted in 1972 against President Nixon. Dissatisfied with Nixon's policy of detente and support of a national family-assistance plan, the American Conservative Union and several veterans of the Draft Goldwater Committee induced Ashbrook to oppose Nixon in the Republican primaries. Ashbrook, an unreconstructed Goldwaterite, never gained more than 10 percent of the vote in any primary; he withdrew from the race in June 1972. Although the weakness of his presidential campaign has often been attributed to the fact that Ashbrook challenged an incumbent of his own party, this explanation is too pat. Eugene McCarthy jolted an incumbent president in the Democratic primaries of 1968 because he found a liberal, antiwar constituency. Ashbrook found no corresponding constituency on the Right: most conservatives could live with Nixon, albeit with a certain amount of grumbling. Indeed some of them—such as Jeffrey Hart, a senior editor of *National Review,* and Patrick Buchanan—wrote speeches for him. The support was not entirely one-sided: establishment Republicans, particularly Nixon, went out of their way to hire conservative journalists. Such people served as liaisons to the embattled Republican Right and helped justify the shifting administration policies to conservative purists.

If postwar conservativism has been a series of movements rather than the orderly unfolding of a single force, the Goldwater campaign is the most crucial turning point in its history. Goldwater's acquisition of the Republican presidential nomination dramatized the political power of the postwar Right. It also mobilized masses of supporters. Before Goldwater's appearance on the national scene, observed William Rusher and James Burnham, there were no more than about a hundred conservative activists, mostly centered on *National Review.*[28] After 1964 there were tens of thousands ready to mobilize behind other conservative candidates for high office. Although this analysis may not take account of the Right-wing campus activism of the late fifties and early sixties, it is correct about the catalytic effect of 1964 in engendering a conservative mass movement.

The Goldwater campaign, however, hurt the older conservatism in two ways: by equating its social philosophy almost entirely with free enterprise; and contributing to a conservative movement more concerned with electoral victories than unifying principles.[29] The multitude of activists, once assembled, became the major force among conservatives. A movement that Kirk, citing T. S. Eliot, hoped would fight for the "permanent things" became increasingly concerned with opinion polls and electoral majorities. And since both the welfare state and coexistence with Soviet tyranny were perceived to be the will of the American people—including a majority of Republicans—conservative activists were forced to seek victory by being discreetly critical of the status quo.[30]

The Nixon Dilemma

In 1968 Governor George Wallace of Alabama, running as a third-party candidate in the presidential race, captured 13.5 percent of the vote. Although *National Review, Human Events,* and other main-line conservative publications interpreted Wallace's support as evidence of popular dissatisfaction with government programs of social engineering, the conservative establishment swung behind Nixon. Wallace's background as both a strident segregationist and a New Deal Democrat who remained a liberal on many issues made many conservatives distrust him. Another factor that contributed to Nixon's conservative support was the established relationship of conservatives to the Republican party. For better or worse, conservative activists and spokesmen were wedded to that party that they had partly taken over in 1964. This marriage continued in 1968, though it required conservatives to affect enthusiasm for a protean politician who in his second term disgraced them and his party. The endorsements of Nixon, which came from Goldwater, from Strom Thurmond (the former Dixiecrat who turned Republican), and from Ronald Reagan, undoubtedly helped make Nixon more palatable to the political Right.[31] Perhaps the same effect was achieved when *National Review,* once openly contemptuous of Nixon, reminded its readers that Wallace was (unlike Nixon) a "big-spending" Democrat.

Despite these assurances, conservative activists by the late sixties had reached an impasse. They had become mere foot soldiers in a party that they had once hoped to control. Even the Nixon loyalist Pat Buchanan complained that under the current administration liberals received the substantive rewards and conservatives only the symbolic.[32] The Wallace constituency of 1968 and 1972 (before the shooting of Wallace during the

Democratic primaries) offered a tempting target for conservative recruitment. Yet Wallace voters were, for the most part, socially conservative New Deal Democrats who were not ready to join the majority of conservative activists as members of the Republican party. Indeed, some of these activists themselves came to doubt what advantage *they* derived from being Republicans. In the 1970s, M. Stanton Evans, William Rusher, and Kevin Phillips explored the possibility of creating a third party that would bring together economically conservative Republicans and socially conservative Democrats.[33] The fusion of Goldwaterites and Wallaceites within a single national party never came to pass, although Republican, and even some Democratic, politicians exploited blue-collar grievances against busing and other judicial remedies intended to end racial inequalities.

Part of the reluctance of conservatives to step unambiguously outside the two-party system came from their conviction that it provided political stability. Even the creation of state conservative parties was justified as a temporary tool, a means of nudging the Republican party toward the Right on social-economic matters. This point was made explicit when the New York Conservative party came into existence. Frank Meyer, upon returning from the Party's first meeting, declared that "conservatives neither desire nor demand clearly wrought ideological parties and are firm, principled supporters of the two-party system." What galvanized the temporary breakaway was opposition to the attempt of the Republican leadership "to make their party as close a carbon copy of the reconstructed Democratic Party of Franklin Roosevelt as it can force upon its Republican constituency."[34] Daniel Mahoney had made the same argument in 1962, in his defense of the New York Conservative party. The new party (really pressure group), by allowing Republicans to vote for conservatives in gubernatorial and Senate contests, would discredit the state Republican leadership. It would restore the state Party to older Republican principles. Moreover, the Conservative party, said Mahoney, would be able to appeal to socially conservative (mostly ethnic Catholic) Democrats who could never bring themselves to pull a Republican lever. Once these voters became used to supporting a non-Democratic party that reflected their real views, they would join traditional Republicans in an expanded Republican party without its Left wing.[35]

Unfortunately, this analysis rested upon the neglect of one overshadowing fact: continued blue-collar, ethnic support for New Deal economic programs, except for those that went almost exclusively to the urban underclass. Kevin Phillips tried to get around this divorce between blue-collar and moneyed conservatives, but his political strategy was based on a highly problematic trade-off. Hoover-type Republicans and Sunbelt Goldwaterites were to abandon anti–New Deal economics in order to build a winning coalition with Catholic Democrats. Yet it remained unclear in Phillips's scheme what free-enterprise Republicans would obtain—beyond a compromised victory—if they renounced their economic principles. Nor was it a sure thing in 1968 that non-Hispanic ethnic Catholics would leave the Democratic party, even in pursuit of pro–New Deal, socially conservative Republicans. Catholic identification with the Democratic party remained high throughout the 1960s—even after factoring out the Hispanic vote. Significantly, Phillips himself was a Republican party strategist. His projected realignment was intended to serve the cause of Republican electoral victory; he dedicated *The Emerging Republican Majority* to the Machiavellian prince whose favor he was seeking, Richard M. Nixon.[36]

The first wave of post-Goldwaterite conservative activism ended as an exercise in futility. Unable to push the Republican party in a conservative direction, it failed equally to obtain leverage among blue-collar, antiliberal Democrats. But the radicalization of liberal politics in America—what appeared to many its assault on patriotism, educational standards, and family values—was already by the early 1970s generating a new wave of antiliberal activism. The new activists were not all Republicans or even defenders of private enterprise. Some were intellectuals with Leftist backgrounds, and others were religionists becoming politically involved for the first time, in response to the abortion issue or the possibility that Gay Bills of Rights might be enacted in their states. Moreover, some of those who had become activists in the sixties began to adopt more sophisticated approaches to political conversion. They set up think tanks, hired statisticians, and produced and distributed position papers. They also attempted to draw scholars long identified, but increasingly disenchanted, with the Left into anticommunist or pro-capitalist foundations.

Delusions of Grandeur

By the seventies, however, many conservative activists had lost their own philosophic bearings. Entering conservative politics after college, they had once dreamed of translating their historical vision into political practice. They had seen that vision vulgarized by the attempt to make it salable to voters. Conservative activists spent years in the antechambers of power, as the valets and messengers of the "country-club Republicans" whom they professed to despise. They became trimmers, because they were powerless and because they had no hope of putting their principles (which they sometimes forgot) into practice. The conservative students and professors who abandoned the universities for the "real world" of politics may well have deluded themselves. In largely turning their backs on the institutions where ideas were transmitted, and by failing to devote themselves more energetically to what M. Stanton Evans prematurely called in 1961 a "conservative revolt on the campus," the American Right withdrew from the battle over principles. The supposedly conservative foundation of the seventies and eighties would generate alternatives to liberal policies, without directly challenging liberal principles and values. In 1985 the favorite presidential candidate of the Republican Right, Representative Jack Kemp of New York, proclaimed equality to be the key conservative principle; he defended democratic capitalism (actually a welfare state economy with capitalist incentives) as the best means for reducing social inequalities. Kemp's political doctrines have much in common with those of the intellectual Left; indeed, political differences between Right and Left have by now been largely reduced to disagreements over policies designed to achieve comparable moral goals.[37]

The Polish émigré novelist Leopold Tyrmand observed that the American Right offered political solutions to cultural problems. He was undoubtedly correct. Unlike the Left in the sixties which entered politics enjoying academic strength and highbrow respectability, conservative activists formed a movement without either. They may have hoped that electoral success would bring intellectual respectability to both them and their world view. For a time, electoral success eluded them; when it found them at last, as we shall argue, they were no longer able to establish the ideological basis of what, by the 1980s, was the conservative counterestablishment.

Chapter Three

Ivory Tower/Ivory Gate:
The Conservative Mind on Campus

The 1960s and seventies were a period of creative ferment for the conservative movement. Issues crystallized, ideas took shape, lines were drawn. These were, to some extent, the issues and ideas that propelled a popular speaker at the 1964 Republican Convention first into the governor's mansion in California, and ultimately into the White House. Despite the brilliance of such political successes, intellectual conservatism suffered massive defeats on the most significant battlegrounds: the institutions and organs of cultural life in the United States, particularly the universities.

It was no secret that liberalism predominated in the postwar academic community. What Lionel Trilling described as the "adversary culture" had been on the increase throughout the century. In 1959 a *Harvard Crimson* poll of undergraduates revealed that two thirds of the students supported the welfare state status quo, while up to a third supported the socialization of basic industries and the unilateral suspension of atomic bomb testing.[1] Of course, the indications were not entirely unambiguous. The late fifties also saw an increase of conservative student organizations. In 1961 the conservative columnist M. Stanton Evans was so encouraged by the signs of discontent that he titled his book *Revolt on Campus*. In a chapter ominously named "Chicago 1960," he gave a glowing report on the Youth for Goldwater and predicted, quite correctly, Goldwater's successful bid for the nomination in 1964. Still, as Evans admitted, there was not yet a "massive shift" to the right, and he conceded that his own interpretation of the students' political mood was at variance with the conventional wisdom.[2]

Campus Revolt

It would be tedious (and unnecessary) to rehearse all the events that disturbed the serenity of college life in the sixties and early seventies. A number of generalizations, however, may be in order. First and foremost, it is important to recall the circumstances. Campus unrest was not, by and large, a response to conservative principles, because such principles were in short supply in academic circles. On this point, Evans was absolutely correct. The faculty and administrators of the sixties ranged, on a political spectrum, from liberal supporters of the New Deal to radicals of every description. Nathan Pusey, who was later forced to resign as Harvard president after using the police to dislodge student protestors, had earlier professed enthusiasm for campus radicalism as a sign of intellectual ferment. Academic supporters of Lyndon Johnson were typically derided as reactionaries. Republicans were beyond the pale.

Even the Eisenhower years may not have been quite the return to "normalcy" that was advertised. The restoration of American ideals, which characterizes the postwar years, was to some extent constructed by popular writers like Walter Lippman and the Catholic theologian John Courtney Murray, and by image-makers like Henry Luce, the publisher of *Time* and *Life*. As Allan C. Carlson, one of Luce's admirers, expresses the mission of *Life* magazine: "*Life* would not merely reflect and defend values; it would create values for the new social, political, and cultural environment that appeared to be emerging in America. Luce determined to shape a spirit for his age, one that would be compatible with a new era and still be in service of the good in America's past." In this, the American century, the United States found itself in danger of losing its soul because of the new responsibilities and temptations that presented themselves. In his view, Americans had to resist godless communism while at the same time celebrating its past and looking toward a bright new future. For the stability it needed, the country would have to depend on the family-centered culture of the suburbs and the moral teachings of generic religion.[3]

In one sense, the 1950s were nothing more than a temporary sigh of relief after the troubled decades of depression and war. The adversarial radicalism of the thirties was still deeply entrenched in academic soil. In their study of the 1972 election, Ladd and Lipset sum up the results of a series of academic surveys, all of which show that throughout the twentieth century, "the political weight" of academics has been to the Left.[4]

Second, the campus revolution was largely an upper-class affair. Students were sensitive only to fashionable segments of the underclass but openly hostile to blue–collar workers. Michael Lerner, a former student radical, complained of the double standard by which the "respectable bigotry" of "an upper-middle-class peace matron toward a lower-middle-class mayor" is not scrutinized with the same care as a policeman's bigotry towards blacks.[5] The most prominent radical group, Students for a Democratic Society, was a predominantly upper-middle-class organization. At a time when family income in the United States averaged $8,000 a year, and the Harvard family average was $17,000, Harvard SDSers came from families averaging $23,000 a year. Stanton Evans's informal survey of conservative students (taken about 1960) pointed to family income of only about $5,000.[6]

Finally, many students who took part in demonstrations were motivated as much by high spirits, the onset of spring, and the feeling of student solidarity as much as by any political principles, even as low a principle as fear of the draft. If the "movement" was not especially threatening to the peace of the commonwealth, the reaction of respectable academics, who were confronted by rioting students, was an understandable alarm. Much of the reality-mugging (to use Irving Kristol's phrase) that sobered up anticommunist liberals took place on campus.

The campus "revolution" began, roughly speaking, with the Berkeley Free Speech Movement and crested with the violent shutdown of Columbia. Response among serious scholars varied. At Berkeley, a young professor, John Searle (now an eminent philosopher), saw little to object to in the Free Speech Movement, although he did point out that the political students utterly rejected the standard definition of the university as a place of teaching and research.[7] For Searle, and many others on both sides, the problem was not so much politics as academic order. The doctrine of *in loco parentis* was dead (at least at state universities), but, as Searle suggested, "so far no new ideology has really replaced" the older ideology.

If Searle was blasé, older scholars like George F. Kennan were appalled. Kennan's Swarthmore speech, "Rebels Without a Cause," was a harmless enough encomium on the ideal of academic detachment, but, when it was printed in the *New York Times,* it aroused such a storm of controversy that a book was made out of Kennan's speech and the hostile responses it had generated. (Martin Duberman at Princeton referred to "gross misrepresentation . . . barely a sentence . . . free of false accusation.")[8] Many distinguished academics like Nathan Glazer and Sidney Hook went farther than Kennan in deploring the threat to academic order at Berkeley and elsewhere. Their reaction marks a significant turning point in the creation of a neoconservative worldview.

Anticommunist liberals were deeply disturbed by the young barbarians who interrupted their classes, but many conservatives (if the truth be told) took a certain melancholy pleasure in the whole business. For years, Richard Weaver, Russell Kirk and Thomas Molnar had been lamenting the disintegration of academic order and intellectual integrity. Now, their worst fears were being realized. Kirk's articles on higher education, which appeared regularly in *National Review,* took on an uncharacteristic briskness and topicality. In 1978 Kirk wove his speeches and articles into one of his most cogent books, *Decadence and Renewal in the Higher Learning.*

The conservative indictment against higher education was sweeping. Several points were made repeatedly: standards—of instruction and civility—had been lowered; the university had lost all sense of its original purposes; conservative ideas were excluded from most departments of political science, history, philosophy, English, and sociology. Russell Kirk saw the contemporary history of higher learning as the annals of "progressive decadence." The old classical vision of "justice, liberty, order, piety" was replaced, by 1955, with an "amorphous humanitarianism" which, "though it had badly damaged the old disciplines, had created no decent curricula to replace them. The unpleasant insecurity of many colleges by 1955 was produced, in part, by this very lack of form and purpose."[9]

For many conservatives, then and now, the principal problem was one of standards. Thomas Molnar, in a bitter and often brilliant book, *The Future of Education,* argued that despite the enormous gains in population since the nineteenth century, the actual number of educated Americans had, at best, remained constant. Throughout the fifties and sixties, Jacques Barzun—a liberal traditionalist—pilloried the follies and pretentions of *The House of Intellect* and lamented the fallen state of *The Teacher in America.* In the former work, Barzun recounts the failure of his graduate students to identify twenty common abbreviations or tell the difference between "i.e." and "e.g.": "What a commentary on so-called preparation for graduate study that these trifles . . . should not have been mastered long since. . . . One is tempted to conclude that our present 'approach' (for it is not a system) turns out with certainty only two products—complaints and cripples."[10]

Albert Jay Nock had made an even more extreme case for "excellence" years before and endorsed Jefferson's plan of public education by which "twenty of the best geniuses will be raked from the rubbish annually."[11] The expected answer to such reactionary criticism was, as Nock and Barzun knew, the charge of elitism. The disciples of John Dewey were educating children to be citizens in a democracy, while the conservative view of learning applied only to a small minority of aspiring aristocrats.

To some extent, conservatives accepted the charge. Russell Kirk, more generous than Nock (or Jefferson), pointed out that universal college education actually hurt both the bright and the dull student: "In the academic mob of 1967, the better students were frustrated, for general standards had been lowered beneath their interest and capacity. In this academic mob, the inferior students were bewildered and baffled, for even degraded standards were too high for them."[12] When the question of excellence began to be raised again in the 1980s, it was always expressed in democratic terms. The influential editors of a conservative blueprint for the humanities, *Against Mediocrity,* now are content to couch their arguments in a prudently egalitarian style and speak of the humanities as "the strongest democratizing force that formal education can muster" and even as a "birthright" for all Americans.[13] In less than twenty years, the conservative argument had become, apparently of necessity, egalitarian.

The argument over standards reveals an essential confusion over the actual purpose and functions of higher learning, as Adam B. Ulam explained in his contribution to a *Daedalus* symposium on higher education.[14] The most popular vision of the university was that of University of California President Clark Kerr, who promoted the idea of the "multiversity." The vulgarity of Kerr's vision is summed up in the term he invented. Its popularity among academics—during the very period Berkeley was coming apart at the seams—was a clear indication of the identity crisis in higher education.[15] John Searle at Berkeley was willing to settle for the old formula of teaching and research, but (as Barzun and others were arguing) few universities wasted much time worrying about undergraduate teaching, which ranked near the bottom in a 1965 survey on "University Goals and Academic Power" conducted by the American Council on Education. (The highest ranked goals were academic freedom and institutional power.)[16] Beyond the two eminently worthy goals of teaching and research lay an equally serious matter: character development. What sort of men and women, what sort of citizens would be produced by a university education?

Two answers were given throughout the 1960s—one liberal, one radical. Harvard President Derek Bok, who presided over Harvard's "restoration," simply dismissed the problem of character development on the grounds that "we have no way of knowing." Academic virtues, he argued, include such things as intellectual skills, "qualities of mind," and developing something he calls "judgment and values" which a liberal arts education can encourage by, for example, offering "the opportunity . . . to experiment with a number of interests and life-styles."[17] A liberal education, with the accent on liberal, provides students with opportunities to become themselves, whether that "self" be Albert Einstein or Charles Manson.

Radical critics of the university, following in the footsteps of Marcuse, accused administrations of repressing creativity and individuality. Paul Goodman, in *Growing Up Absurd,* set the tone for much of the radical critique. One can almost hear Goodman's influence in the once-popular book *The Student as Nigger,* whose author, Jerry Farber, declaims against school as the place "where you let the dying society puts its trip on you."[18] In their quest for liberation, such students were, in the view of psychologist Carl R. Rogers, creating "the person of tomorrow." The men and women of the future would reject all orthodoxies (including marriage) in favor of turning themselves on by whatever means they had. On the other hand, they would reject the liberals' dispassionate pursuit of truth. The Person of Tomorrow would be "active—sometimes violently, intolerantly, and self-righteously active—in the causes in which he believed."[19]

The Conservative Response

Conservatives were repelled by the violence and obscurantism of radicals and Marxists, but they agreed with them (against the liberals) that universities did, and should in principle, serve a moral purpose. The explicitly moral purpose of education is an ancient ideal, far older than Plato. The Roman rhetorician Quintilian summed up the ancient attitudes in his famous definition of the orator as "a good man skilled in speaking," that is, a man capable of moral judgment and public service. A handful of traditional scholars continued, right through the 1960s, to adhere to the old view, but they were rare birds in academic circles. In both issues of the *Daedalus* symposium, Gerald Else (a classical scholar) was one of the few to suggest that education's essential purpose was not to produce graduate students but "to train our students to make better moral and political choices."[20]

Apart from Russell Kirk, the conservative most identified with issues of higher education was John A. Howard, president of the tiny Rockford College and a member of President Nixon's Task Force on Higher Education. In the Task Force report "Priorities in Higher Education," Howard registered his dissent from the recommendation for increased federal spending. He who pays the piper calls the tune, he often warned. Rockford College under Howard, along with Hillsdale College in Michigan under George Roche and Brigham Young University, made valiant efforts to stem the rising tide of federal control over higher education. As Howard, Roche, and Kirk all warned, the dependence on government money eventually translated into acceptance of government priorities and guidelines that were set, typically, by bureaucrats and educationists who had no clear idea of the function of higher education.

In a debate with the Marxist H. Bruce Franklin, Howard insisted that it was a serious error to restrict the university's mission to "the pursuit of truth." There had to be a framework of principles, a system of "character education," if the other aims of education were to be reached.[21] While they disagreed on almost everything else, Howard and Franklin did agree that education had a social and moral purpose beyond mere intellectual and vocational training.

Few academics were listening to Howard's plea, although a number of groups like University Professors for Academic Order were founded to provide a conservative answer to the campus problems. Most serious professors, however, were too busy worrying about the threat to academic freedom posed by campus radicalism. Wayne Booth, who described the university as "the last true church," expressed strong indignation when he heard that New Left students were tampering with the University of Chicago library's card catalog. "The Shrines are under attack," he declared in his essay "The Last True Church."[22] Corroborative testimony was provided by three distinguished legal minds, including the future solicitor general Robert Bork, in their 1970 congressional testimony. Primarily concerned with the legal implications of campus politics, Bork and his colleagues went on to complain that the conditions for research were undermined by incivility and political polarization. Despite the divisions and tensions of academic life, they argued, "Politicization has . . . produced an opposite danger, that of conformity."[23]

Academic Freedom

In fact, throughout the sixties and seventies (and up to the present) conservative ideas and those who advanced them have often been shouted down by the radical opposition. After a 1971 *Atlantic* article on the genetic basis for I.Q., Harvard Professor Richard Herrnstein fell victim to a campaign against "racism" (the article never discussed race) by SDS. Other victims of the crusade against genetics and I.Q. included Arthur Jensen and the admittedly eccentric William Shockley. (A debate between Shockley and black activist Roy Innis was canceled in 1973 as the result of radical protest.) James Q. Wilson, a moderate liberal authority on crime and society, was subjected to a similar campaign, and his views may have cost him his chance to become Harvard's Dean of Arts and Sciences. During the same period, Harvard's economics department began caving in to pressures to hire more Marxists.

In some cases, the radical coercion turned brutal. Edward Banfield, author of the influential study of urban problems *The Unheavenly City,* was hounded from a chair he had accepted at the University of Pennsylvania and had to return to the comparatively civil world at Harvard. The neoconservative scholar (and ambassador to the United Nations) Jeane Kirkpatrick was driven off the stage by radical students in the course of her Jefferson lecture at Berkeley in 1983. Similar incidents have marred the academic serenity of Northwestern, Smith College (where a Kirkpatrick lecture had to be canceled), and Howard University, where ex-Black Panther Eldridge Cleaver tried to exhort black students to regard themselves as Americans. While most decent liberals deplored such disruptions, others preferred to ignore the discomfiture of their enemies. Even after the horror of the campus uprisings, University of Massachusetts President Robert Wood could find no threat to academic order on the Left. Instead, he complained against Jensen, Herrnstein, and Banfield on the grounds that they signified "the emergence of the first intellectually respectable school of conservative thought since the antebellum South's George Fitzhugh."[24] Wood's remark was all the more curious since he seemed totally unaware of such movements as the New Humanism, the Southern Agrarians, the "new" conservatives of the 1950s, and the free-market economics of the Austrian school and Milton Friedman. Such a degree of ignorance (or ideological passion) in a university president would seem to confirm the conservative impression that, to use Booth's phrase, the shrines were not simply under attack: they were already occupied.

The fear and hatred that greeted the hardheaded analysis of Herrnstein, Banfield, and James Q. Wilson was manifested, time after time, whenever "conservative" ideas disturbed the peace of college campuses. When the leading sociobiologist Edward O. Wilson attended the 1978 meeting of the American Association for the Advancement of Science, he was met with snarls of "racist" and "Nazi," before a bucket of water (or worse) was dumped on his head. The difficulties encountered by these scholars and scientists were predictable, since their research of the late twentieth century can be construed as a direct challenge to the liberal view of human life that held sway in the academic community.

Academic Heresy

In many ways, the postwar years were a period of extraordinary intellectual ferment in the United States and Europe, especially in the sciences that study man. Up through the 1940s and fifties, a sort of orthodoxy could be discerned in the social sciences and moral philosophy—an orthodoxy that would receive a series of powerful shocks from scientific rebels. The major schools of thought—behaviorist psychology, John Dewey's psychological and educational theories, Boasian anthropology, Sartrean existentialism, liberal and Marxist political theory—represented a high degree of consensus on the nature of man. Human nature was largely an open-ended affair, determined neither by biology nor history. The mind was viewed, by many social scientists, as essentially a Lockean "tabula rasa," a blank slate on which experience could create any conceivable message.

History became a sort of enemy, an obstacle to be surmounted in man's progress toward a better future. Democratic values—liberty, equality, and social justice—came to be viewed as things in themselves, rather than competing values, while the history of the United States became less and less a narrative account of previous generations and their accomplishments and more and more of an Hegelian search for meaning in the historical process.

Throughout the twentieth century, colleges and universities had been at work redefining their roles. What had been, in the nineteenth century, a community of scholars sharing the wisdom of the past with young students, was gradually transformed into an uneasy combination of research lab and indoctrination center. The classical academy and John Henry Newman's Christian concept of the university had come to be seen as largely irrelevant. A new democratic America required socially responsible citizens, not priests or aristocrats with a smattering of classics. By the early 1950s, colleges and universities had become the symbolic expression of the highest aspirations of industrial America. The reigning orthodoxy had survived challenges from the Left (Marxism) and the Right (the new humanism and agrarianism). Anticommunist progressive liberalism was *the* social and political philosophy of American intellectual life.

John Dewey, in many ways the most prominent American philosopher of the early twentieth century, combined a blank-slate psychology with a commitment to liberal democracy and social progress. He did not entirely rule out the effect of drives or instincts, but they were only "raw materials" for which "custom furnishes the machinery and designs." This meant, in effect, that human beings were capable of almost infinite progress toward a more just and humane society. A similar message was preached by the father of behaviorism, John B. Watson, and his disciple, B.F. Skinner. Watson reduced human instincts to three emotions: fear, love, and rage. Everything else was determined by environmental stimuli. Skinner advanced the behaviorist argument in several significant directions: First, he took up the question of language, which he treated as a simple case of stimulus and response, that is, language is only an instrument for satisfying desires; second, he promoted a utopian view of social and political life in his novel *Walden II* and in more theoretical works in which he argued that human social behavior could be improved simply by redesigning the environment.

These utopian psychological notions derived added force from the anthropological theories of Franz Boas and his students, Margaret Mead, Ruth Benedict, and A.L. Kroeber, among others. The Boasians emphasized the notorious variability of human cultures which gave the human species an "exemption from heredity."

Politically, these arguments gave support to Marxists, who repeated Marx's dictum that "man is the creature that makes his own history"; to existentialists, who argued that human beings created themselves; and to social reformers, who looked forward to endless vistas of humanitarian progress. In every real sense, then, the politics of the postwar welfare state was bound up with a scientific worldview that can be conveniently described as environmentalist.

An attack on utopian environmentalism was mounted in several disciplines: (1) the rise of cognitive science in linguistics and psychology; (2) the coalition of social science and evolutionary biology that came to be known as sociobiology; and (3) a new tough-minded approach to social problems that began to surface in sociology, educational psychology, and economics. In only a few cases were the rebels actually aware of any political implications to their work, but in each case, the scientists and scholars who put forward the new theories were attacked, sometimes physically, not so much on the grounds that they were wrong, but because it was morally wrong even to discuss certain questions.

The Cognitive Revolution

The rise of cognitive sciences has taken place in a number of separate, apparently unrelated disciplines: linguistics, psychology, computer science, and anthropology. The late 1940s and early fifties were a period of crisis for scholars and philosophers who concern themselves with the mind. None of the various schools of psychology had succeeded in establishing its principles as *the* main program for the discipline. The dominant school, behaviorism, focused almost exclusively on external patterns of behavior. This concentration effectively blocked any consideration of mental life. As Karl Lashley pointed out in a famous address, human beings, like all organisms, have a nervous system that responds *actively* and constantly to the stimuli it receives. Work on information theory (leading up to the construction of electronic computers) also emphasized the specific technique by which information could be processed, but it was Noam Chomsky who put cognitive science on the map. [25]

Chomsky made his mark early with a review of B.F. Skinner's *Verbal Behavior.* [26] Arguing against the mechanical view that reduces language to patterns of stimulus/response and networks of habit, Chomsky insisted upon the "creativity" of all human behavior, language in particular. Not long before his review, Chomsky had published his first major work, *Syntactic Structures,* in which he worked out the first version of his theory of generative grammar. In later works like *Aspects of the Theory of Syntax* and *Language and Mind,* he drew out the psychological implications. Going against the grain of most linguistic and psychological theory, Chomsky insisted that there are structures in language (syntax, for example) which are universal. What is more, he insisted, there are formal universals that underlie and determine the rules of native languages. Chomsky has repeatedly revised almost every aspect of his theoretical work, but he has continued to emphasize the innateness of mental structures.

In psychology, Jerry Fodor comes close to representing the extreme "nativist" position. Fodor argues that the everyday language we speak—

"natural languages"—cannot be the language of thought, because in that case we could not have had access to the thought processes we need to acquire a natural language. Put simply, learning English would be impossible if our minds did not somehow have a universal language built into them. Experiments conducted by cognitive psychologists, while they are not conclusive, do show that the mind tends to learn in some ways and not in others.[27]

Some of the strongest arguments against the blank state come from an unexpected quarter: color perception. Color terms do, in fact, vary from language to language. The general assumption has been that most cultures perceived color differently from Europeans and Americans. Recent studies, however, seem to show that color-vocabularies and color-perception are biased toward discriminating the four basic colors: blue, green, yellow, and red. What is more, even people without any color words are able to learn a "natural" vocabulary (i.e., one that discriminates the basic colors) twice as quickly as an unnatural. The naturalness of the basic colors is physiological, since the retina is designed to be roughly sensitive to the wavelengths that correspond to blue, green, yellow-green.[28]

Emotions are, perhaps, more obviously universal. Cross-cultural studies indicate a degree of agreement on interpreting facial expressions: happiness, anger, fear, surprise, and disgust can be correctly guessed from pictures of facial expressions. Even children born deaf and blind exhibit a standard repertory of expression. What is more surprising, many chimpanzee facial expressions can be correctly interpreted by students.

It now appears that such essential features of perception as constancy of shape and size and object permanence are present in newborn children, and cannot, therefore, be acquired by experience. Newborns also seem programmed to respond to the human face and voice (especially female), and children—when they are first beginning to talk—display a knowledge of grammar (with their very first words) never attained by chimpanzees that have been trained to communicate.[29] There are obvious implications for a conservative worldview. Human mental life and (by implication) social institutions are not infinitely plastic: they are rooted in the structures of the mind which is, itself, conditioned by the organic development of the brain. Few (if any) conservatives took note. Noam Chomsky was mentioned only in connection with his radical politics or, even more rarely, in attacks on the use of transformational grammar in the schools.

The New Synthesis

The implications of cognitive science were not lost on Edward O. Wilson, the Harvard entomologist who coined the term sociobiology.[30] For much of his career, Wilson has devoted himself to studying the social insects. Increasingly he came to apply the central insights of Darwinian natural selection to social behavior. In essence, modern Darwinists argue that every aspect of an organism—its body, sensory and mental abilities, and social behavior—evolved under the pressure of competition. Sharper teeth, better vision, and mating patterns are the result of a contest between individuals with different sets of genes. The winners are those which reproduce at higher rates; their genes eventually come to dominate or take over the population. Wilson was on fairly safe ground politically until, in the last chapter of *Sociobiology: The New Synthesis,* he turned his attention to the human species.

Obviously, Wilson was not the first writer to describe human behavior as the result of natural selection. It has long been believed that our distinctively human way of living is the result of a struggle for existence. The Christian view of human nature is very similar (although many Christians would prefer to speak of the old Adam or original sin). Even before Darwin wrote *The Origin of Species,* the philosopher Herbert Spencer was explaining human social life as the survival of the fittest. Ever since, "social Darwinists" have used what they knew (or thought they knew) of human origins to explain the current conditions of human life. Unfortunately, a corrupted version of social Darwinism got taken up by racial theorists whose works were exploited by the Nazis. The resulting contamination rendered the subject almost untouchable for nearly two decades. Serious interest in the human implications of evolutionary biology did not revive until the 1960s, with the publication of *On Aggression* by the ethologist Konrad Lorenz, *The Imperial Animal* by the anthropologists Robin Fox and Lionel Tiger, and the popular books of the playwright Robert Ardrey: *African Genesis, The Territorial Imperative,* and *The Social Contract.*

Of these pioneers, Lorenz is by far the most important. Before taking up the human question, he had a distinguished career as a student of animal behavior—for which he received the Nobel Prize. *On Aggression* is a study of aggressive impulses in a number of species. Man, so Lorenz argued, was not by nature a particularly violent creature, especially against members of his own species. As a result, we lack the necessary mechanisms to regulate it. However, when men became hunters and warriors, they had to rely on their uncontrolled aggressive impulses. For this reason, according to Lorenz, we need such cultural institutions as clearly defined lines of authority (rank order or hierarchy) and rituals (sometimes religious) to defuse our violent impulses once they have been aroused.

Others of these early writers—most notably Ardrey, Fox and Tiger, and the zoologist Desmond Morris—compared human behavioral patterns with what is known of other primates, especially the baboons that live in large troops. They painted an unattractive picture of males domineering over females, fighting to establish pecking order, and defining and maintaining territorial boundaries. Man is, to use Desmond Morris's title, a "naked ape," or in Ardrey's phrase, the "killer ape."

The scientific community did not take seriously the writings of dramatists and anthropologists. Lorenz was a different matter, but—it was whispered—in his youth Lorenz had expressed sympathy for Hitler's eugenics policies and the German racial laws. However, by the early 1970s, a number of researchers were taking a new approach to certain facets of animal behavior. W. D. Hamilton, Robert Trivers, E.O. Wilson, and Richard Dawkins were looking at such phenomena as sex ratios among social insects (e.g., bees and wasps) and the question of altruism from the perspective of genetics. In principle, they argued, animal behavior should contribute to the reproductive success of the individual. This meant, in effect, that one set of genes was winning out in a competition with other sets. Therefore, the willingness of an animal to risk its life (or even sacrifice it) should be related to the amount of genetic material they had in common, that is to their degree of relatedness. (Years before, the geneticist J.B.S. Haldane had been asked in a pub if he would lay down his life to save a brother. No, he replied, not for *one,* but he would do it for three brothers or nine cousins. The point of his joke is simply this: I share with a brother—or parent or child—50 percent of the same genes and with a cousin 12.5 percent. By saving three brothers or nine cousins, I shall actually be enhancing the reproductive success of my genes.)

Richard Dawkins offered the most radical statement of this position in *The Selfish Gene* and *The Extended Phenotype.* For Dawkins, everything is in the genes. Organisms are simply vehicles which these replicating bits of DNA have adopted to insure their survival and propagation. Dawkins and his colleagues were fond of quoting a witty remark of the Victorian novelist Samuel Butler that a chicken was just an egg's way of making another egg.

In the minds of most people, the single most important event in the development of this revolution was the publication of Wilson's *Sociobiology: The New Synthesis*. In the controversial last chapter of *Sociobiology* (and in the later *On Human Nature*),[31] Wilson applied the genetic insights of Trivers and Hamilton, as well as his own, to the problems of human society. The book was an overnight success everywhere, except in academic departments of sociology, psychology, and anthropology.

The most controversial question taken up by sociobiologists was the nature of human sex roles. By the 1980s, a great deal of research in psychology, anthropology, and sociology began to converge. Males and females, it began to be argued seriously, possess specialized mental aptitudes. Male students consistently outperform females in certain areas of mathematics, while females appear to excel in verbal skills. Men turn out to be, predictably, somewhat more aggressive, women more nurturant.[32]

This sexual distribution of mental abilities could be plausibly related to the sexual division of labor that was almost universally observed. Studies of family life and child-rearing revealed a greater uniformity than first appearances might indicate. In the view of many cross-cultural anthropologists, women are everywhere charged with primary responsibility for child-rearing and housekeeping, while men typically monopolize such activities as making war and hunting big game.[33]

Feminist scholars in the seventies began to make use of Sherry Ortner's observation that woman is to nature as man is to culture,[34] and a healthy interest in women's studies began to challenge certain liberal assumptions. Women were not always miserable in primitive or patriarchal societies; in fact, some feminists argued, women's place in the world had been seriously eroded by modernization, which laid such great emphasis on the more typically masculine qualities: specialized division of labor and analytical reasoning.[35] Increasingly, many feminists began to realize that the sexual revolution and campus radicalism amounted to little more than denial of women's special needs and rights.[36] Most seriously, liberalized divorce laws had the effect of impoverishing mothers with small children[37] and increasing the risks of child abuse.[38]

Most political feminists rejected such a line of reasoning, even though much of the research was conducted by women, indeed by feminists. Some conservatives, by contrast, were aware of the implications of this research and eager to use it in building up a case against the misapplication of sexual equality. Steven Goldberg, in a deliberately provocative book, argued for *The Inevitability of Patriarchy*. Women, he contended, should abandon their feminist pretentions and "follow their own physiological imperatives." In his view, "women have more important things to do" than compete with men. If feminists insist upon competition, then they will forfeit their right to protection.[39]

George Gilder, a former Republican liberal, argued from a paradoxically feminist perspective that men were the weaker sex because the male identity was a social invention, which could be undermined by feminism. Men, he suggested, had to be tamed by women or they would never make good husbands and fathers. On the other hand, men needed to find fulfillment in all-male groups where they did not have to compete with women.[40]

The Left was not slow to respond to the challenge of sociobiology and sex-role research. The attack on sociobiology reached its peak with the publication of *Not in Our Genes* by R.C. Lewontin, Steven Rose, and Leon Kamin. Jensen and Herrnstein were duly taken to task for their statements on I.Q., and Steven Goldberg was ridiculed for his "engagingly direct" arguments. The authors reserved their most powerful attacks, however, for sociobiology. After going over the usual slurs against Lorenz, Ardrey, and Dawkins, the authors delivered their verdict: "Inequalities of wealth, power, and status are not 'natural' but socially imposed," the standard Leftist position. As for the methods and research data of sociobiology, they are declared "fundamentally flawed."

Since the authors, especially Lewontin, were reputable scientists, their attack (endorsed by Stephen Jay Gould in the *New York Review of Books*) has to be taken seriously. However, resentment as well as research went into their arguments. The discussion of Richard Dawkins is, for example, patently unfair. They distort Dawkin's arguments and go so far as to present as part of his theory certain ideas that Dawkins introduces as the "entertaining speculations" of his colleagues.[41]

In fact, many of the criticisms made by Lewontin and others were previously addressed and answered by Dawkins. The most basic objection is to genetic determinism per se. Stephen J. Gould and now Lewontin, Rose, and Kamin apparently find it morally and intellectually reprehensible to think that there are several genetic constraints on human sexual behavior, although they have few reservations on the score of environmental determinism. On the surface, at least, distinction is political: if men were naturally violent and territorial, if human beings inevitably sorted themselves out in pecking orders, if male dominance really were a natural phenomenon and not just the result of social and cultural oppression, then certain elements of the Marxist political agenda might well have to be reconsidered.

Not in Our Genes (and all the essays and anthologies churned out in the late seventies) was a clear sign that implicitly conservative ideas were not covered by academic freedom. Few conservatives, it should be noted, took up the cudgels for E.O. Wilson or even bothered to examine the debate (Gertrude Himmelfarb is a distinguished exception). Well into the 1980s, the conservative publication *Human Events* continued to print diatribes against "Darwinism." The one conservative philosopher who did make an effort to understand the new science was Thomas Molnar. At first he was attracted to the refutation of environmentalism, but, as he explained in an *Intercollegiate Review* article, he was put off by the scientists' philosophical naiveté and their hints at genetic planning. The "veterinarian" view of human life urged by Lionel Tiger would cancel any idea of moral responsibility: "Conduct for which not the free agent but the phylogenetic imprint is responsible is nothing but a mechanical act. On such an arid ground the moral judgment is pulverized and the political community joins the ant-hill."[42] Molnar's rejection of sociobiology (and Darwinism itself) would be echoed by many less erudite and less intelligent journalists on the right. On his own ground, the Christian view of men and society, Molnar was certainly prudent in rejecting any form of materialism. What he did not see, or rather what he was less interested in seeing, was the full implications of a scientific view of social and cultural behavior that restored a sense of the "givenness" of human nature. Paul Johnson, a British moderate conservative, was one of the few to be deeply impressed. He begins his history, *Modern Times,* with an account of Einstein, whose relativity disturbed the peace of the universe, and he concludes with Edward Wilson, whose sociobiology restored man to his place in nature. Johnson ends his remarkably influential book on a sanguine note: "Was not human planning to produce a 'classless society' not only intrinsically unattainable but positively harmful, in that it conflicted with the hidden but magisterial plans of nature itself? It might. The experience of modern times, when human activism led so often, and on so grandiose a scale, to inhuman destruction, suggested as much. On the other hand, it might not. It was possible human improvement could be used to reinforce natural selection. The essential thing was to find out." Thus by the 1980s, the wiser minds among us had returned to Alexander Pope's conclusion: "The proper study of mankind is man."[43]

Sociological Reaction

A biological reconstruction of sociology was unlikely to win many conservative adherents (apart from racialists); however, sociology itself was another matter. The roots of the discipline, as Robert Nisbet has demonstrated, go deep into the counterrevolutionary thinking of the nineteenth century. While conservatives have generally regarded sociology as an upstart discipline and a willing participant in schemes for social engineering, more than a few important postwar sociologists could be regarded as conservative or even reactionary.

Robert Nisbet is the most obvious example. Both as the philosopher of his discipline in *The Sociological Tradition* and in his works on community and authority, Nisbet revealed himself as one of the most thoroughly conservative scholars in America. There were others. George Homans, one of the founders of small group sociology, pursued an implicitly traditionalist line of research both in his study of medieval England and in his attempt to discover the roots of social cohesion. In his autobiography, Homans finally declares his conservative principles without reservations.[44]

In many ways, Homans's nemesis at Harvard was Talcott Parsons, the most influential American sociologist. Parsons's work is often opaque to the point of unintelligibility, but in the main he supported the postwar restoration of the bourgeois order, endorsing the nuclear family and traditional sex roles, and some of Parsons's students have carried on his affirmation of "the American way of life."[45]

One of the earliest classics of sociology was Emile Durkheim's attempt to relate suicide rates to religious affiliation, and Robert Nisbet and Peter Berger (among others) have recognized the profoundly conservative implications of Durkheim's research. Mention should also be made of Mircea Eliade's magisterial writings on non-Western religions and, more recently, studies by Steven Stack and Rodney Stark, which improve upon Durkheim's original work: belonging to a church now appears to significantly lower an adolescent's chance of committing suicide.[46]

In the 1960s and seventies, many noted sociologists were particularly interested in questions of social and political organization. Seymour Martin Lipset became famous not only for his classic study, *Political Man,* but also for his discussions of union politics, big business, and higher education. Lipset, along with Irving Kristol (and later Nathan Glazer), was coeditor of the *Public Interest.* From its inception in the 1960s, the new journal displayed a deepening distrust of utopian politics and the revolutionary claims put forward by radicals. Even the title conveyed a new respect for the public interest of the nation as a whole, which distinguished it sharply from Marxist and radical sectarianism.

Dismantling the Welfare State

By the 1970s the *Public Interest* had become a rallying point for disaffected sociologists and political scientists who recognized, with Nathan Glazer, the increasing social and economic costs of social engineering. Mention has already been made of Edward C. Banfield's difficulties. His book, *The Unheavenly City*, while it was not written from a conservative perspective, outraged the Left and delighted the Right. Banfield showed, among other things, that many social programs, ostensibly aimed at improving the whole of society (especially the disadvantaged), actually were designed to benefit the relatively affluent: "The expressway program and the FHA and VA mortgage insurance and guaranteed programs in effect pay the middle-class white to leave the central city for the suburbs. . . . These government programs . . . aim at problems of comfort, convenience, amenity, and business advantage, not at once involving the essential welfare of individuals or the good health of the society."[47]

Banfield's criticism of urban planning was shocking enough, but even more controversial was his argument that most racial problems were, in fact, class problems. Each immigrant group has gone through a lower-class phase from which it has worked its way out. The riots of the sixties, which were supposedly in response to racial discrimination, were actually conducted "for fun and profit."

A good liberal on most social questions including race, Banfield's book was offered as a progressive criticism. One by one, other honest liberals were to come forward with similar criticisms. In *Visible Man* and *Sexual Suicide* (1973), the still-liberal George Gilder documented the effects of the welfare system on poor blacks, an insight developed a decade later by Charles Murray into a thoroughgoing critique of poverty programs, *Losing Ground,* a book that became the primary topic of conservative conversations in 1984–85.

The works of Gilder, Murray, and Harvard professor (later United Nations ambassador and senator) Daniel Patrick Moynihan drew attention to the plight of female-headed black families. Many black scholars, somewhat surprisingly, were already making similar arguments. In *The Declining Significance of Race,* University of Chicago sociologist William Julius Wilson provided compelling evidence that as upwardly mobile blacks separated off from the community, class was becoming a more important factor than race. Thomas Sowell, a black economist, has repeatedly pointed to the paradoxical effect of social policies. Sowell, like Walter Williams and activist Robert Woodson, has argued that government programs designed to help the urban poor (blacks especially) have proved to be the greatest obstacle to black social progress. By creating habits of dependency, removing the rewards for effort, and providing disincentives for family stability, federal and state governments have served to establish a permanent underclass.

Economics is the cutting edge of social analysis, and it is in economics that the impact of conservative ideas has been greatest. The success of Milton Friedman and George Stigler, among many others, is all the more surprising when the apparently universal triumph of Keynesian economics is taken into consideration. In the mid-1930s, Friedrich von Hayek was engaged in a losing struggle against Keynes. For the next fifty years he took refuge in the obscurities of capital theory and, increasingly, devoted his best efforts to political philosophy. Both classical economics and the Austrian school, with their emphasis on individual decision-making, seemed dead beyond hope of recovery. By the 1950s, however, Milton Friedman was giving a twist to the Keynesian tail in such works as *A Theory of the Consumption Function.* By the early sixties he was reaching a broader audience, which he initiated into the values of free men in free markets. Friedman seemed tireless, not only in reviving the "quantity theory of money" but also in promoting his own favorite alternatives to the planned society: a voucher system for education and a negative income tax.[48] His study of monetary policies led him to conclude that the federal reserve brought on the Great Depression by its incompetent tinkering with the money supply.[49] Friedman's sometimes simplistic social philosophy is summed up in the title of his television series, *Free to Choose.*

Free choice became a unifying theme of much economic theory in the sixties and seventies. James Buchanan and Gordon Tullock, first in their book, *The Calculus of Consent: Logical Foundations of Constitutional Democracy,* and later through their journal, *Public Choice,* attempted to apply economic theory to decision-making outside the marketplace. In their view, much of what government does is an illegitimate usurpation of individual choice. At times approaching close to libertarian anarchism, the Public Choice school has hammered on the need to constrain the role of government. Buchanan has pointed out that economic theory, by using maximizing models of analysis, encourages planners in their assumption that the economy can be managed. Markets are, in fact, less precise than textbooks suggest. More importantly, interventions into the market must be based on some social philosophy of common good—a philosophy generally rejected by individualists.

George Stigler, like Friedman, a Nobel Laureate, also contributed to the critique of social planning. In papers and lectures on economic regulation, he maintained that regulatory agencies inevitably act in the interest of producers, rather than consumers, while suggesting more than once that students of economics were inexorably attracted to conservative ideas.[50] Other prominent economists who began to unravel the seamless garment of the welfare state included economic historian Douglass North and Armen Alchian; on a more abstract level, Robert Nozick exerted a powerful influence in the direction of free choice and responsible citizenship. While Nozick's libertarian ethics were unlikely to appeal to older social conservatives, his *Anarchy, State, and Utopia* served as a rallying point for intellectuals disenchanted with the growing power of the state.

On several fronts—psychology, sociobiology, social analysis, economic theory—conservative ideas were on the advance in the postwar years. Ironically, many conservatives were at the same time abandoning the field to their enemies. Some conservative intellectuals were forced out by the new McCarthyism; others chose careers in politics or political journalism. Few of them seemed very concerned with passing on the torch to another generation. In a letter to *Chronicles,* one of the rare birds—a real conservative with a successful academic career—Grace Goodell, expressed her misgivings:

As a "conservative" social scientist now with tenure in a major academic institution, I have found that the stultifying intellectual atmosphere—institutionally and interpersonally, though certainly not in print—which the older generation of mature conservative thinkers have themselves created for the younger generation coming along, has been far more discouraging at almost every step of my own development than have liberal and leftist antagonisms. . . .

Listening to conservative students at various of the leading college and university campuses, one is tempted to generalize that the most antisocial professors teaching young people today are almost invariably those of conservative persuasion—especially of that generation. In my years at college and through graduate school, even on post-doctoral grants, from campus to campus conservative professors stood out as a group for their closed doors and intolerance even toward genuinely conservative students. Rather than seeking out or at least welcoming young minds of sincere inquiry, like Solzhenitsyn, many of our mentors seem to us to have retreated with undiscriminating arrogance—perhaps self-protection, self-pity, and bitterness?—behind a siege blockade, while we, the young seeking to prepare ourselves to carry on the challenge of our age, were left on the outside of the barricades.[51]

Of greater significance, perhaps, was the steady withdrawal of conservative scholars (apart from economists and neoconservatives) from the mainstream of academic debate. As time went on, more and more seemed to devote their energies to writing articles in conservative magazines, less and less to carrying on the fight within their disciplines.

There were, of course, conspicuous exceptions, especially among historians: the cold war historian John Lukacs, constitutional scholar Forrest McDonald, Southern regionalists Ludwell Johnson, Clyde Wilson, and Grady McWhiney. But by 1980, the year of Ronald Reagan's accession to the presidency, conservative scholars of rank and influence were in short supply.

The pursuit of political influence comes at a price: the loss of academic prestige. A new Republican administration was, at times, hard put to locate conservative appointees with solid academic credentials. When qualified conservatives were suggested for positions at the NEH or the Department of Education or for the National Archives, they were quickly shot down by the overwhelmingly liberal academic community. The most prominent casualties included M.E. Bradford, who failed to win nomination as director of the National Endowment for the Humanities (and later as national archivist). By 1986 it was clear that Reagan supporters of the highest distinction would not be allowed to serve in any position requiring Senate confirmation. Among those rejected for National Humanities Council positions were Charles Moser, a professor of Slavic languages and literatures with solid credentials, and E. Christian Kopff, an important classical scholar with an impeccable record. Both were dropped by the White House for their conservative views on such matters as Marxism, homosexual rights, education, and feminism. Despite the success of conservative ideas on campus, conservatives themselves had become an embittered and marginalized minority.

Chapter Four

Revolt of the Intellectuals:
The Neoconservatives

The 1970s were a decade of severe crisis for American conservatives. The landslide reelection of Richard Nixon, which was supposed to usher in a new Conservative consensus, quickly provided the opportunity for liberal Democrats to take the offensive during the Watergate hearings and their aftermath. In the mid-seventies the dissolution of the Republican party was being confidently predicted, as conservatives turned increasingly to Ronald Reagan and moderates attempted to regroup around safe party leaders like Jerry Ford and Howard Baker.

What hardly anyone expected to see was the emergence of two new conservative forces that would influence the presidency of Ronald Reagan, while at the same time alarming the remnants of the Old Right. These two forces were the neoconservatives and the populist and religious New Right (discussed in the next chapter). Both groups have created or refashioned institutions and publications to articulate their views, and both have been remarkably successful—albeit in different ways—at raising money and attracting the attention of the press.

Breaking Ranks

It is true but simplistic to state that as American academics and journalists moved Leftward during the civil rights crusade and the Vietnam War, the conservative mainstream drifted in the same direction. The reality is more complex. As American universities, literature, and art became increasingly radicalized from the mid-sixties on, cold war liberals, those dissatisfied with black power politics, and, finally, critics of what became known as the "counterculture" all disengaged from the Left. This process of disengagement among incipient neoconservatives has been described exhaustively from different angles, by Peter Steinfels and Alexander Bloom on the Left, by an admiring English scholar Gillian Peele, by George Nash in his survey of the conservative movement, and by two leading neoconservatives, Norman Podhoretz and Irving Kristol, in their autobiographical writings. The critical moments in this flight from the Left are related by major commentators in a similar fashion. Although Kristol (often described as the neoconservative "godfather") has had the greatest success in formulating the movement's aspirations in a set of formal doctrines, it is Norman Podhoretz, editor of *Commentary,* who has become its most representative figure.

As a culturally conscious young intellectual, Podhoretz had temporarily abandoned his Truman-Democratic (cold war liberal) politics to become a protester against the Vietnam War. As an editor of *Commentary* in the 1960s, he had pulled a magazine that had been founded in the early fifties as a pro-Israeli, anti-Soviet publication toward the emerging New Left. In *Making It* and *Breaking Ranks,* Podhoretz dwells on his onetime fascination with Freudian critics of capitalism, such as Norman O. Brown and Herbert Marcuse, and with other heralds of the counterculture.[1] His break with the Left occurred by stages, which are documented in his editorials for *Commentary.* Podhoretz rediscovered the evils of Communist rule and expansion and, furthermore, grew disgusted with the Left's attacks on academic standards and the principle of merit (as illustrated by its demand for preferential treatment of blacks and women). Podhoretz also turned against the revolution in sexual and social relations that counterculture writers were advocating in the sixties and seventies. The effect of the new morality on family life and already confused adolescents was a theme Podhoretz and his talented wife, Midge Decter, discussed with increasing urgency throughout the 1970s. A *Commentary* leitmotiv for the 1970s was established in the December 1970 issue, which included several articles criticizing such spokesmen for the counterculture as Charles Reich and Theodore Roszak, both of whom had written against repressive, middle-class morality.[2]

Among the factors that led Podhoretz and many other neoconservatives to disengage from the Left, their Jewishness was certainly significant. From 1969 on, *Commentary* included strongly worded polemics that presented the "Movement," particularly black radicalism, as a danger to American Jews.[3] Critics like Earl Raab and Nathan Glazer stressed the inevitably anti-Jewish character of the policies advocated by the New Left and its liberal followers. An anti-Israeli policy closely keyed to Arab revolutionary organizations, the willful neglect of Jewish victims of Soviet oppression, and the catering to black demands for preferential hiring in the New York City school system and elsewhere were all features of the movement that Podhoretz and his associates castigated. Isidore Silver has made an observation about the Jewish consciousness of neoconservatives, which Alexander Bloom, in *The Prodigal Sons,* has recently drawn out at length:

Although psychohistorical explanations have substantial, built-in limitations, it is apparent that the development of neoconservatism in the last twenty years has consisted of a reaction to one major trauma—the fear of anti-Semitism. Since, of course, not all Jewish intellectuals are neoconservatives nor are all neoconservatives Jewish, a conventional disclaimer of universality should and must be entered. Despite the caveats, however, there can be little doubt that the Holocaust constituted the seminal event not only for European Jewry but for many American Jews not far removed from their East European or German heritages.[4]

Silver makes the argument that the neoconservatives were impressed by Hannah Arendt's *Origins of Totalitarianism,* particularly by her discussion of the populist and tribalist roots of modern anti-Semitism. Arendt had traced both totalitarianism and anti-Semitism to the inability of the ruling classes in France, Germany, and the Slavic countries to retain their legitimacy in the face of upheaval and mass political movements. To the neoconservatives who had fought their way to the top academically, while being confronted with professional obstacles, the danger lay exactly where Arendt had claimed it was, in lower-class populist jealousy.

But anxieties over populist upheaval have not always led to the same political views. Though similar concerns can be ascribed to other American Jews, most of the American Jewish community, and particularly its more affluent and better educated elements, continues to identify with the liberal Left. The majority of American Jews may see their enemy in a Christian rural America from which it seeks protection through an enlightened managerial state and progressive judiciary. The Jewish neoconservatives, in any case, have not yet swayed a critical mass of Jewish voters, however much they and their coreligionists may agree about specifically Jewish issues.

Despite the close and enthusiastic identification of *Commentary* with the Reagan administration (Norman Podhoretz's son-in-law, for example, serves as an assistant secretary of state), President Reagan obtained a smaller percentage of the Jewish vote in 1984 than in 1980. The 70/30 split of the Jewish vote between Walter Mondale and the president did not at all reflect the electoral preferences of Jewish neoconservatives.[5] Moreover, a poll conducted by the American Jewish Committee (which sponsors *Commentary*) in 1984 revealed that 70 percent of the Jewish respondents oppose silent meditation in schools, 87 percent favor "gay rights," and 80 percent support federally funded abortions. None of these positions coincides with the dominant *Commentary* views, though the respondents and Jewish neoconservatives may both have experienced problems related to their Jewish identity.[6]

Many Jewish neoconservatives now find themselves in unfamiliar circumstances, as the unavoidable allies of a political movement that until now has been predominantly Christian. In this situation they are justifiably sensitive to any outbreak of anti-Semitism on the Right. In the summer of 1986, an acrimonious quarrel erupted between several New York–based neoconservatives—most prominently Norman Podhoretz, Midge Decter, and Dorothy Rabinowitz, a columnist for the *New York Post*—and Joseph Sobran, a senior editor of *National Review*.[7] Sobran, for some time, had published critical statements about the role of Zionists in American political life and about Jewish hostility toward Christian society. Sobran had even had the temerity to praise *Instauration,* a journal devoted to scientific racism, for its willingness to broach risky opinions about social relations. The neoconservative reaction was predictably impassioned: It ranged from demands to have Sobran professionally blacklisted to cries about virulent anti-Semitism on the Old Right.

Fighting on Two Flanks

In fact, the fight did reveal understandable tensions between the neoconservatives and some elements of the Old Right. While the neoconservatives have generally added luster to conservative organizations, one effect of this alliance has been to shift the parameters of conservative respectability toward the center. Positions significantly to the right of *Commentary* are increasingly regarded as suspect. Southerners and Christian traditionalists have been particularly suspect to the neoconservatives, who during Reagan's first term fought successfully to keep M.E. Bradford from becoming director of the National Endowment for Humanities. Although such animosity may be explained in terms of philosophic differences, it is impossible to rule out cultural factors entirely. Bradford represents a Southern agrarian point of view that neoconservatives equate—quite unfairly in most cases—with anti-Semitism and rural reaction.[8]

If some members of the Old Right have come into conflict with neoconservatives, the Left has been even more openly hostile to the same group. Sidney Blumenthal of the *Washington Post* has produced a book in which he seeks to document the careerism of those neoconservatives prominent among pro-Reagan journalists and within the Reagan administration. Though Blumenthal claims to be examining the rise of the entire "conservative counterestablishment," it is obvious that both his strongest dislike and deepest interest are directed toward neoconservative renegades from the Left.[9] Christopher Hitchens has covered much of the same ground, without anecdotal embroidery, in a biting article in *Mother Jones.* Here, amid caricatures of neoconservative celebrities, Hitchens details the political and professional honors and connections of Norman Podhoretz and his family.[10] Podhoretz, besides directing *Commentary,* is on the board of directors of the international anticommunist Committee for the Free World, a founding member of the Coalition for a Democratic Majority, a member of the Committee on the Present Danger, and a syndicated columnist for the *New York Post.* His wife, too, has served as an editor of *Commentary* and is active in the same anti-Soviet defense-minded organizations as her husband: Committee for the Free World, Coalition for a Democratic Majority (a group composed of erstwhile supporters of the late Senator Henry Jackson), and Committee on the Present Danger. Midge Decter is also on the board of directors of Heritage Foundation and former senior editor of Basic Books. John Podhoretz, the son of Norman and Midge, is an executive editor of *Insight,* the weekly magazine of the *Washington Times,* and an editor of the increasingly neoconservative monthly, *American Spectator.* One Podhoretz son-in-law, Steve Munson, has served as a director of the Committee for the Free World and has edited the influential neoconservative periodical *Public Interest.* Munson has worked as press counselor for the neoconservative celebrity Jeane Kirkpatrick while she was U.S. representative to the United Nations; he is currently news specials chief for the Voice of America. The other Podhoretz son-in-law, Elliott Abrams, worked on the staff of Senator Daniel Moynihan and was an assistant secretary of state for human rights. He is now the highly visible assistant secretary of state for inter-American affairs.

The power and connections of what their enemies sometimes called the "*Commentary*-crowd" appear even more impressive as the family tree moves to Irving Kristol, former managing editor of *Commentary,* coeditor of *Public Interest,* and publisher of *National Interest.* Hitchens notes Kristol's ties to the American Enterprise Institute, the *Wall Street Journal,* and the Committee for the Free World, and his former association with Basic Books and the English journal *Encounter.* He misses Kristol's ties to the Olin Foundation, including his occupancy of the Olin chair at New York University, given almost entirely for his private research. Ernest van den Haag, Kristol's friend, occupies another lucrative Olin chair in the Fordham University Law School. Hitchens extends the neoconservative family tree to Jeane Kirkpatrick, Ben Wattenberg, Max Kampelman (the chief U.S. negotiator at the Geneva arms talks), and other prominent public figures.

Creating a Counterestablishment

While Leftists grumble at these examples of empire-building, neoconservatives have in fact created their own opportunities. To their great credit, Kristol and the Podhoretzes turned *Commentary* from a culturally parochial New York periodical into one read and discussed by the president, his advisors, and foreign heads of government. The appointment of Jeane Kirkpatrick as U.S. representative to the United Nations occurred after Ronald Reagan had read her November 1979 *Commentary* essay, "Dictatorships and Double Standards." President Reagan's recent calls for the establishment of liberal democracy throughout the world closely parallels another theme that *Commentary* has played up. [11]

Kristol, Podhoretz, and Wattenberg have managed to surround themselves with impressive academic talents. *Public Interest* and *Commentary* feature in every issue such outstanding scholars of public policy as Daniel Bell, James Q. Wilson, Edward Banfield, S.M. Lipset, Aaron Wildavsky, and Nathan Glazer. Daniel Patrick Moynihan remained closely attached to friends at *Commentary* from the time he was professor of sociology at Harvard until his election to the Senate in 1976. Although Moynihan subsequently veered to the Left, he nonetheless hired incipient and declared neoconservatives—such as Chester Finn, Joshua Muravchik, and Stephen Miller—to work on his senatorial staff. The senator has also published blasts against anti-Zionists and the Old Right in *Commentary* and *Public Interest.*

The bicentennial issue of *Public Interest* testifies to the academic luster that neoconservatives have brought to their enterprises. The issue includes essays by Bell, Glazer, Lipset, Wilson, and S.P. Huntington, all scholars with Harvard connections, another essay by Moynihan, and a study by the constitutional scholar and political neoconservative Martin Diamond.[12] Kristol, Wattenberg, and Podhoretz have been able to channel much of the same talent into other neoconservative publications, especially *Public Opinion, This World,* and the *Wall Street Journal.* They helped Hilton Kramer launch the *New Criterion,* a journal that expresses their cultural and political approach to aesthetics. This elegantly produced periodical features highly gifted interpreters of art and literature such as Joseph Epstein, Samuel Lippman, Bruce Bawer, and Kramer himself. Its defense of what might be described as anticommunist, prodemocratic modernism has brought down charges upon the editors of being crass political reductionists. The *New Criterion* is well-edited and includes such notable academic contributors as Robert Nisbet and Edward Banfield. Moreover, unlike other journals devoted to interpreting art, music, and poetry, it is admirably open about its political values.

At their best, neoconservatives have brought to the intellectual Right a critical intelligence that has proved useful in political discussion. Although members of the Old Right grappled with legal theory and economics, they rarely sought the kind of statistical confirmation that neoconservative academics produce for their positions. The editorial staff of *National Review* opposed court-ordered busing in the 1960s by appealing to the original meaning of the Fourteenth Amendment and by arousing popular resentment against the government's interference with established community life. The neoconservatives, Glazer and Banfield, criticized the same experiment by documenting its failure to achieve the intended result. Busing did not lead to increased racial harmony or to improved scholastic performance for black or white children.[13]

In an incisive commentary on the differences between the paleo- and neoconservatives, Edward Shapiro has stressed the critical importance of their methodological points of departure. The paleoconservatives drew their insights and convictions from a humanistic and religious heritage. Although they studied economics and law defensively, in order to protect inherited institutions, their hearts remained in literature and theology.[14] The neoconservatives, by contrast, revel in statistics and computerized information. They believe that social problems are amenable to rigorous investigation that can throw light on them and thereby contribute to their solution. While not all neoconservatives are better trained than all paleoconservatives in the methods of the social sciences, Shapiro is correct about the dominant attitudes of both groups. What paleocon-servatives often attribute to human frailty, or to the failure to deal ade-quately with that condition, neoconservatives treat as problems for which there exist right and wrong solutions. Neoconservatives may cry out in despair about the intractability of anti-Semitism, terrorism, and the So-viet empire. They may, as Irving Kristol did in an essay for *Partisan Review,* praise T.S. Eliot's later, Christian poetry. Yet, their position is not entirely incompatible with modern state planning. Almost all neo-conservatives, and certainly the distinguished academics among them, remain qualified defenders of the welfare state. This loyalty is under-standable in light of their study of society as sets of problems, which may or may not call for state action. One need not search far in the work of Glazer, Moynihan, Lipset, Wildavsky, or Wilson to find proof of what Michael Oakeshott calls "rationalism in politics." All of them believe that social problems can be properly managed if the state acts on the basis of knowledge.

This line of thought crops up occasionally even in Irving Kristol, whom Russell Kirk describes as "not a neoconservative at all . . . but a Con-servative." In his *Reflections of a Neoconservative* and elsewhere, Kristol lists among neoconservative doctrines the support of a "conservative welfare state." Kristol distinguishes this kind of regime from both the night watchman state advocated by libertarians and democratic and non-democratic forms of socialism. It is obvious from his descriptions that he is referring to the present American model of a mixed economy and a bureaucratically managed democracy. Kristol defends that model in his acidic commentary on David Stockman's *The Triumph of Politics,* pub-lished in the *Wall Street Journal.* He scolds Reagan's former budget di-rector for the simpleminded belief that the Reagan revolution originally aimed at rescinding the welfare state.[15] The proper task of the current administration and of any other conservative one is to prune the over-growth of an essentially sound form of government. George Will, a close friend of Kristol's and a self-declared Tory Democrat, notes scornfully of the Old Right that "people who preach disdain for government can con-sider themselves the intellectual descendants of Burke, the author of a celebration of the state." Further: "Two conservatives (Disraeli and Bis-marck) pioneered the welfare state and did so for impeccably conserva-tive reasons: to reconcile the masses to the vicissitudes and hazards of a dynamic and hierarchical industrial economy."[16]

The same belief in the welfare state shapes the neoconservative de-fense of the family and of other intermediate institutions between the individual and the state. Identified with, among others, Peter L. and Brigitte Berger, Michael Novak, and Allan Carlson, neoconservative plans to assist the family are based on the view of the welfare state as being a useful as well as necessary condition of life. The battle to preserve the family from disintegration is to be waged through the state, by revamping taxes and transfer payments to favor two-parent families, natality, and domestic stability. In all fairness, it must be said that Allan Carlson, one of the most vigorous defenders of the traditional family allied with the neoconservative camp, has begun to argue against the welfare state as well as "the ideological corruption of social work." Carlson has arrived at the view that the welfare bureaucracy is irreversibly opposed to established social morality. Family services, he argues, must be "reprivatized" in order to save what remains of lower-income families from total restructuring at the hands of social engineers. Carlson's pessimism about the family under the managerial state connects him more closely with the New Right than with neoconservative sociologists. In a November 1985 essay for *Commentary,* Peter L. Berger, perhaps the premier sociologist of religion and emphatic defender of the nuclear family, extols the "gigantic political efforts to ensure that no group within it [America] is excluded from the cornucopia of industrial capitalism." Looking toward the future for even further progress, Berger calls for "a specifically American version of the welfare state" without the bureaucratic obstacles that have hindered similar enterprises in Europe.[17] This statement is particularly illuminating in view of the fact that the Bergers have been relentlessly critical of most family assistance programs that have originated on the Left.[18]

Undoubtedly the neoconservative view of the welfare state stems partly from a recognition of the historically given. At this point it seems unlikely that the system of transfer payments, poor relief, and extensive commercial regulation that operates in American society, with bipartisan political backing, will ever be substantially reversed. Kristol may indeed be correct in how he interprets the support for Reagan's pledge to "get government off people's backs." The voters took this pledge, says Kristol, as a promise to trim government and lower taxes, not as a restatement of Goldwater's plan to rescind the welfare state. But if George Gilder is correct in describing neoconservatives as principled, not merely calculating, defenders of a mixed economy and managerial state,[19] then the neoconservatives' belief in the welfare state is both a permanent aspect of their ideology and a characteristic that distinguishes them from the older Right.

Neoconservatives also distinguish themselves from older American conservatives by their vision of a global democratic order. Although this vision is one that Irving Kristol views critically and Jeane Kirkpatrick approaches with reservations, it is nonetheless basic to the thinking of other neoconservatives. This neo-Wilsonian focus has been evident in the foreign policy pronouncements of Norman Podhoretz, Ben Wattenberg, and Elliott Abrams and may have moved from them and other *Commentary* writers into the speeches of President Reagan. Some of the younger neoconservatives, most notably Joshua Muravchik, Michael Ledeen, and members of the National Endowment for Democracy (which serves as a bridge between organized labor and the neoconservative camp), advocate a global democratic revolution.[20] Such a revolution is to lead to a worldwide secular, politically egalitarian community. In the short run, non-Western governments are to be encouraged to hold democratic elections and to undertake land reform, unionization, and capital formation. The entire world is to be brought into conformity with the American regime that has developed in the twentieth century. A November 1985 *Commentary* symposium on America since 1945 makes abundantly clear that prominent neoconservatives (Kristol is the most notable exception) do not typically search for their ideals in the past. Whatever problems they find in present-day America, they marvel at how far it has come since 1945 in achieving more democracy and social justice. This was the point of a series of television lectures by Ben Wattenberg a few years ago; it is also the theme of a recently published book of his that describes high divorce rates and other apparent signs of social decay as more or less the fruits of newly won freedoms.

Neoconservatives present themselves as political centrists who deplore the lack of moderation on both sides of the spectrum. In *Breaking Ranks* Podhoretz depicts himself as supporting the moderate progressive candidate for the Senate, Daniel Moynihan, against the Left-wing extremist Bella Abzug and the equally extremist incumbent Senator James Buckley.[21] Diane Ravitch, whose writings on educational problems have appeared in *Commentary*, has claimed to occupy the same middle ground. Miss Ravitch seeks to save public education from the Right, which demands "ideological and moral purity," and from the Left, which promotes "far-out ideologies of sexual liberation."[22] Although her writings are usually more critical of progressive educators and sex education than of creationists and anticommunists, her sense of symmetry is characteristically neoconservative. Neoconservatives, who may have learned from

Arthur Schlesinger's book by that title the value of claiming to be the vital center, never abandon, at least rhetorically, the *juste milieu.*

Moral and tactical reservations about their association with the older Right have led neoconservatives into producing their own account of a conservative movement that is anticommunist and patriotic but also humane and moderate. Such a conservatism, according to this account, did not arise through *National Review.* In fact, William Buckley had to tame his own magazine to bring under control the "seedbed infested with racism, chauvinism, and paranoid looniness" that Suzanne Garment in the *Wall Street Journal* identifies with the older Right.[23] Although, according to this view, "you can still hear an echo of the Right's more distasteful origins" in the pages of *National Review,* Buckley and his associates have "pried conservatism from the fingers of its more demented followers." In this sense, that journal and its editors are seen as the beneficiaries rather than sources of sound political teachings.

Few neoconservatives ever admit to being deeply influenced by a paleoconservative. Neoconservatives are, however, rich in praise of those mentors with whom they wish to be identified. Irving Kristol pays tribute to Leo Strauss, the German political philosopher, but not to James Burnham, as a father of his movement.[24] Kristol's concept of political realism has much in common with Burnham's, and he has praised *Suicide of the West* in conversation, though not in print. Moreover, Kristol may have been overgenerous to Strauss in attributing to him his own preference for Aristotle over Plato and for Locke over Rousseau. Lionel Trilling, a distinguished longtime professor of English at Columbia, enjoys an almost legendary status among older neoconservatives. Norman Podhoretz, who was Trilling's student at Columbia, invariably describes him with reverence; what is more, Trilling's widow, Diane, is a respected contributor to *Commentary.* Podhoretz and Bell see Trilling as someone who incarnated civility, one of the values considered indispensable for discourse in a democratic society. Podhoretz is particularly impressed by Trilling's attempt to combine in his own life democratic beliefs and cultural refinement. Although Trilling was a Jewish intellectual long mesmerized by Marx and Freud, he wrote critically about the "liberal mind" and warned against the beginnings of the counterculture.[25]

Alexander Bloom has tried to argue that it was not Trilling so much as the less elegant and certainly pluckier Morris Raphael Cohen who helped to shape the neoconservative style. Cohen never made it out of City College of New York into the more prestigious philosophy department at

Columbia. Though he blamed his professional frustrations on anti-Semites, his real problem may have been his combative personality. In this sense, Cohen may have had more in common with Bell, Lipset, Kristol, and other neoconservatives than did the aloof and oracular Trilling. Moreover, Cohen was a fierce anticommunist while Trilling, despite his stately demeanor and Victorian prose, took years to extricate himself entirely from Marxism.[26]

In light of the serious differences between neo- and paleoconservatives, it may seem remarkable that conservative foundations have been receptive to the newcomers. Part of the answer may be found in the quest by conservatives for intellectual as well as political respectability in the face of electoral defeat and isolation from the academic community. The disengagement of prestigious academics and political journalists from the Left opened up the possibility of an advantageous alliance for "policy-oriented" conservatives. By ignoring the divisive issues, pragmatic conservatives hoped (and still hope) to entice into their camp great names from Harvard, Berkeley, and Columbia. Conservatives have also developed more positive attitudes toward Trilling, Adlai Stevenson, and Harry Truman. *National Review* has extolled all three since the early seventies as neoconservative heroes who, had they lived long enough, would by now be on the American Right. Some old conservatives also believe that the entire Right may benefit from neoconservative arguments against the Left and the libertarians. During the late sixties and early seventies, traditionalists were battling anarcho-capitalists who, like Murray Rothbard, called for a minimal state and for an end to defense spending. The old conservatives, Russell Kirk and Robert Nisbet, were (and remain) more critical of libertarians than of neoconservatives.

The old conservatives run the risk of being swallowed up in the alliance that they initiated and sustained. From the mid-sixties on, many of them became convinced that by going into politics or by running foundations, they would promote their ideas more effectively. They began to look to others to represent them both in institutions of higher learning and in highbrow culture. A division of labor was to occur—at least in the minds of some old conservatives. The new breed of conservative activists would pursue political place and lay the financial foundations of a conservative counterestablishment, while academic and literary converts from the Left would fight the intellectual battles.

Conservative activists eventually lost the power to distinguish conservative from nonconservative reasons for the very policies they advocated. In opposing the Equal Rights Amendment, for example, one writer in *Policy Review,* like the president of the United States, avoided the quintessentially conservative argument that sexual roles are necessary for the functioning of a stable society; and prohibition of their political and public recognition is therefore harmful to humanity. Others embraced Nathan Glazer's critique of minority quotas as inconsistent with the 1964 Civil Rights Act and with the individualism that Glazer associates with American democracy. The conservative humanistic perception of the same problem (which can easily be drawn out of the essays of Kirk, Nisbet, and Gertrude Himmelfarb) is much different: It is based on a view of unchanging human nature and on various authorities, from Aristotle to Burke. Conservatives (excluding libertarians) believe in the corporate nature of man; and though they may oppose the further intrusion into society by social engineers in the form of minority quotas, they defend traditional group identities as necessary for the nurture of the individual.[27]

The relationship between conservatives and neoconservatives has nonetheless not been without difficulties. Tensions have surfaced in the 1980s that are more likely to grow than diminish. The symposium on America since 1945 that appeared in *Commentary*'s November 1985 issue stirred latent resentment among old conservative intellectuals. The *Commentary* symposium included people of the Left but, with the exception of Robert Nisbet, featured no one to the right of the neoconservatives. Most of the neoconservative contributors emphasized social progress, even while deploring high crime rates and the Soviet military buildup. The symposium elicited two stormy responses. One was in an issue of *Intercollegiate Review* published by Intercollegiate Studies Institute; here old conservative intellectuals, including Russell Kirk, M.E. Bradford, and George Panichas, the literary critic, presented their predominantly bitter assessment of the neoconservatives. The Southern conservative historian Clyde Wilson expressed a dominant theme when he wrote: "First of all, we have simply been crowded out by overwhelming numbers. The offensives of radicalism have driven vast herds of liberals across the border into our territories. These refugees now speak in our name, but the language they speak is the same one they always spoke."[28]

An even more dramatic sign of Old Right revolt against neoconservative hegemony came in April 1986 at the annual meeting of the Philadelphia Society in Chicago. The Philadelphia Society had originally been set up by Don Lipsett as a forum for debate and discussion among conservatives. The early meetings had often resonated with lively exchanges between libertarians and traditionalists. Frank Meyer and Kirk, surrounded by their followers, had held forth on their differing views of liberty and authority. In the seventies, Philadelphia Society sessions became more subdued; and except for some of the regional meetings at which Harry Jaffa and M. E. Bradford debated the status of equality as a basic principle of the American regime, the organization, and certainly its leadership, tried to give the impression of a broad consensus on the Right. During the Reagan presidency, this theme of consensus became particularly important; conservatives of all kinds saw an opportunity to rule that they were not about to sacrifice as the result of internal division.

In 1985, however, M. E. Bradford became president of the Philadelphia Society and thereafter served a two- rather than one-year term. The gesture seemed harmless enough since the organization had ceased to generate controversy, and, in any case, conservatives who had deserted Bradford for the neoconservative candidate Bennett during the race for the NEH directorship were hoping to conciliate an old friend. But in 1986 Bradford did the unexpected. He staged a debate between conservatives and neoconservatives at the Philadelphia Society at which blood was drawn. Harsh words were exchanged by the participants; and the moderate representatives on both sides were overshadowed by the more combative ones. Stephen Tonsor, a Catholic conservative, declared that Christian Aristotelianism was integral to any true conservative perspective; he deplored the arrogance of former Marxists and radicals dictating policies and beliefs to those who had never strayed from the truth. On the other side, R.E. Tyrrell, the editor of the *American Spectator,* lashed out against "phony conservatives" who had come to divide the Right. Such people, said Tyrrell, had no idea of how much "neoconservatives were suffering for the cause." But that, argued the paleoconservatives, was the point at issue. In their view, neoconservatives had received mostly benefits from their hesitant and qualified identification with the political Right. On the other hand, the Christian Aristotelianism—or neo-Thomism—that Tonsor considered essential to the intellectual Right had never been more than a minority position among postwar conservatives. The exchange at the Philadelphia Society did, however, yield one truth: The growing tension between paleo- and neoconservatives could no longer be disregarded.[29]

The Counterestablishment

The most frequently reiterated complaint against the neoconservatives came down to the simple questions of money and power. For years conservatives had wandered in the wilderness, but now, just as they were about to reap the reward for their suffering, a set of "Johnny-come-latelies" were taking the lion's share. From the early 1970s, self-identified neoconservatives had, in fact, developed close ties with the Scaife, Smith Richardson, and John M. Olin foundations. All of these institutions, which have devoted their resources to upholding traditional American values, have become reliable sources for funding neoconservative (as well as other conservative) enterprises. The Hoover Institution, the Heritage Foundation, and the American Enterprise Institute also include neoconservatives among their trustees and resident scholars. Significantly, all three of these think tanks, which have multimillion dollar annual operating budgets, began as vehicles for Old Right movement conservatives. Originally their publications and the speeches of their staffs represented the foreign and domestic policies associated with *National Review* and with the Goldwater presidential bid.

By the mid-1970s, the direction of these organizations was changing perceptibly. The American Enterprise Institute, founded in 1943, showed the way in the seventies by offering support and fellowship to liberal academics whose collaboration it sought in presenting certain policy positions. Its Council of Academic Advisors and *Public Opinion,* its chief periodical, today work hard to maintain a reputation for academic respectability and political moderation. Ben Wattenberg and Seymour Martin Lipset, the editors of *Public Opinion,* exemplify the American Enterprise Institute's changed orientation. Both came from urban intellectual environments and combine principled anticommunism with strong residual sympathy for social democratic ideals.

The Hoover Institution, which is tied, through an increasingly problematic relationship, to Stanford University, has made similar efforts to obtain centrist respectability. Since the 1970s, and perhaps even since the 1960s, when W. Glenn Campbell became its current president, it has aimed at incorporating main-line academic support. Hoover has also offered generous and extended fellowships to anticommunists of the old moderate Left, such as Sidney Hook. The Heritage Foundation, under the direction of Edwin J. Feulner, formerly with ISI, has searched even more resourcefully for new allies. Since the late seventies, Feulner together with the editors of *Policy Review,* a quarterly published by Heritage, have highlighted foreign, economic, and administrative policies (particularly eschewing divisive philosophical and ethical questions).[30] In this tendency, Feulner and his staff have not broken entirely new ground. Certainly a "policy-oriented conservatism" could already be seen in Goldwater's presidential campaign and among postwar libertarians of the

Right. Heritage, moreover, has maintained important ties to the old Right by naming Russell Kirk one of its senior scholars. (AEI bestowed a similar honor on Robert Nisbet.)

Heritage has used the avoidance of theoretical issues to broaden its appeal among groups that were offended by the Old Right. It has done this while continuing to enjoy the financial backing of Joseph Coors, Jr., and of other staunchly Old Right benefactors. The result of this quest for academic friends on the part of conservative foundations had led inescapably to a new ideological mix; although some foundation leaders persist in treating the postwar conservative movement from 1945 to the present as a seamless robe, even a cursory reading of *Public Opinion* or *Policy Review* would temper their confidence. Proposals for "trimming" the welfare state have replaced plans to dismantle the New Deal. The model for dealing with the Soviets became Truman's "containment policy" or the Wilsonian vision of world democracy, not James Burnham's program of rolling back the Soviet empire by appealing to historic nationalities. Harry Truman, FDR, and Martin Luther King, Jr., were treated with respect, while, by contrast, such heroes of the Old Right as Edmund Burke, Richard Weaver, and Robert Taft were hardly mentioned. Joseph McCarthy survived only as an object of obloquy.[31]

In the 1980s neoconservatives began to face opposition in their handling of foundations. This has happened most noticeably in the case of the American Enterprise Institute, which in 1986 was forced to reduce its full-time staff from 154 to 110.[32] AEI had initiated its opening to the Left under its founder and first president, William Baroody, who had actively sought the collaboration of neoconservative academics for what Baroody has assumed were essentially conservative policies. Under his son and successor William Baroody, Jr., the foundation had tried to build bridges to political celebrities of all types, and it became known as a meeting ground between neoconservatives—such as Jeane Kirkpatrick, Irving Kristol, Ben Wattenberg, S.M. Lipset, and the legal expert Walter Berns—and those further to the Left. Unfortunately for AEI, the organization became progressively less distinguishable from more liberal foundations such as the Brookings Institution. Brookings opened its door to neoconservative policy-experts and thinkers precisely as AEI was drifting Leftward. In 1986, a decision supported by the younger Baroody to invite Vladimir Posner, the Soviet spokesman, to speak at the institute as a guest, angered conservative benefactors. The John M. Olin and Smith Richardson foundations expressed unwillingness to give further support to the straying institute. Although both of these foundations were willing to befriend the neoconservatives, Baroody's behavior had become so distasteful to those who provided the funds these organizations earmarked for AEI that their relationship was entirely severed and Baroody's days at the helm of AEI were numbered.

Despite the defunding of AEI and the flare-up of old conservative resentment against the neoconservatives, it seems premature to speak of a waning neoconservative influence on the American Right. Adam Meyerson, the shrewd young editor of *Policy Review,* has made the useful observation that no group on the Right is a likely candidate to replace the neoconservatives as framers and exponents of policy positions.[33] The old conservative activists have fallen between two stools; abandoning the theoretical interests of the founding generation of postwar conservatism, they then failed to achieve authoritative status as policymakers or policy-experts. Those who are in government or at foundations often play second fiddle to neoconservatives or to authentic New Rightists. The only second-generation old conservatives who will leave their mark on the times may be those who continue to wrestle with ideas and values. Typically, they write for scholarly journals and contribute to the Intercollegiate Studies Institute's *Modern Age* or the Rockford Institute's *Chronicles: A Magazine of American Culture,* while remaining outside of political affairs.

The Old Right may resent what neoconservatives have done with their cause, but for at least the foreseeable future will be in no position to do anything about it. The choices that are available to them are to wage an unpromising struggle or to do what some editors of *National Review* have already begun to do, to blur the distinction between paleo- and neoconservatives—or to pretend that none exists. A third more stoic alternative is also available to the Old Right. It is represented by George Panichas, the editor of *Modern Age,* a Christian Platonist, and a morally committed interpreter of modern literature. Troubled by the thoroughgoing politicization of the intellectual Right, Panichas has warned against the "contaminating" obsession with making it in Washington. He has stressed the distinction between Plato's attempt to spiritualize the political and the modern tendency to reduce spiritual questions to political ones. In his contribution to the *Intercollegiate Review*'s symposium on the state of conservatism, Panichas laments the "sad paradox that conservative leaders and thinkers often fail, in the present climate of their political victories, to recognize or implement their spiritual identity and responsibility.

No authentic conservative metaphysic can be operable when the discipline of God and the discipline of the soul have been ceded to the *doxai,* the dialectical structures and superstructures of modern life." This statement includes an admonition as well as a lament. Old conservatives may eventually come to heed both—out of despair as much as conviction.

Chapter Five

Populist Rebellion: The New Right

The political movement known as the New Right has a great deal in common with neoconservatism. Both movements took formal shape in the 1970s, although their antecedents are much older. Both arose in reaction to what was regarded as a betrayal of purpose. For the neoconservatives, it was Democrats and young radicals who corrupted the great liberal tradition; for the New Right, the villains were moderate Republicans who betrayed the interest and principles of the great majority of ordinary Americans. Both have been remarkably successful at raising money and establishing public-policy organizations, and both are accused of taking over organizations.

For many political analysts, the New Right amounts to little more than "a collection of general-purpose political organizations" in alliance with conservative politicians.[1] These analysts cite groups like the Conservative Caucus headed by Howard Phillips, the Moral Majority (now Liberty Foundation) led by Jerry Falwell, the Committee for the Survival of a Free Congress under Paul Weyrich, the National Conservative Political Action Committee under Terry Dolan, and, to a lesser extent, the Heritage Foundation, which had its origin on the border between Old and New Right, but which has grown over the years into a central conservative organization.

If there are many similarities between the two groups of new conservatives, there are also profound differences. For one thing, many (if not most) of the New Right leaders were previously involved in conservative politics: Richard Viguerie worked for YAF, which he helped to put back on its feet economically; Howard Phillips was an assistant to the chairman of the Republican National Committee and headed the Office of Economic Opportunity under President Nixon; Paul Weyrich had been an aide to Senator Gordon Allot, a conservative Republican; and Phyllis Schlafly was the author of *A Choice, Not an Echo,* a book that galvanized many in the Draft Goldwater movement. Some have gone so far as saying that the difference between the Old and New Right is "purely chronological"[2] or only a matter of the personalities involved.

The continuity is significant. Both groups oppose communism, support free enterprise and limited government, and respect (although they do not always practice) religion and "traditional values." But while the Old Right continues to emphasize anticommunism and free enterprise, the New Right has learned how to emphasize themes that are more populist than conservative: the fear and resentment of the Eastern "establishment," defense of family and conventional morals, popular control over schools and churches. They also display a greater willingness to use single-issue campaigns, like the Panama Canal treaty or abortion, as the basis of external fund-raising.

Richard Viguerie, long the symbolic leader of the New Right, views style and strategy as the binding forces of his diverse movement. He lists four common characteristics of the New Right: technical ability in promotion and politics, a cooperative spirit, a commitment to principle over and above loyalty to the Republican party, and, finally, the optimism displayed in his own title, *The New Right: We're Ready to Lead.*[3] Viguerie is a suitable symbol for the movement he heads: a hardworking, self-made man from the Sunbelt, he is distinguished neither by his learning nor by his literary style. Compared with a William Buckley or Jeffrey Hart, Viguerie resembles a car salesman attending, uninvited, a formal dinner.

Perhaps the single most important element in the success of the New Right coalition was the involvement of Evangelical Christians, including the prominent Evangelists Jerry Falwell and Pat Robertson. The Christian Right contributed more than religious fervor and moral commitment: by the 1980s Christian broadcasting was reaching millions of television viewers and radio listeners, who responded to its appeal for moral revival and patriotic dedication. The impact of religious broadcasting is especially strong in Southern states which increasingly play a key role in elections.

Origins of the New Right

Richard Viguerie dates the formation of the movement he has mid-wived to August 1974, when Gerald Ford selected the liberal Republican Nelson Rockefeller to be his vice-president. It was not simply that Ford had passed over a number of attractive conservatives, but that in picking Rockefeller, Ford had "revealed the true colors of so-called 'moderate' Republicanism by choosing the very symbol of everything we Conservatives had always opposed." Viguerie assembled a group of friends to discuss ways of stopping the appointment. Though they failed to stop Rockefeller, they did succeed in launching a new political movement. This incident and its aftermath underscore several New Right themes: the feeling they had been betrayed by the Eastern establishment; a willingness to oppose the Republican leadership—even in the very difficult days after Watergate; and the use of strategic planning sessions.

The major actors in the early days were Paul Weyrich, Howard Phillips, Terry Dolan, and Viguerie himself. Weyrich had been instrumental in creating the Heritage Foundation and, with the backing of brewing magnate Joseph Coors, established the Committee for the Survival of a Free Congress in 1974. He had previously been active in the American Legislative Exchange Counsel (ALEC) and the Republican Study Committee. Weyrich's Free Congress was instrumental in supporting the election of conservative candidates in the late seventies and early eighties, while disseminating ideological materials through the Free Congress Research and Education Foundation.

In the first decade of his operation, Weyrich succeeded in attracting several valuable collaborators to his banner. Kathleen Teague, a former YAF activist and executive director of the American Legislative Exchange Council, became his board chairman, and conservative Catholics Patrick Fagan, Joseph Piccione, and Patrick McGuignan have all played a significant role in socially oriented projects like the Child and Family Protection Institute.

Connaught Marshner, also a Catholic conservative activist like Weyrich himself, played an important role in focusing attention on issues of education and the family. Author of *Blackboard Tyranny,* coeditor (with Weyrich) of *Future 21: Directions for America in the 21st Century,* chairman of the National Pro-Family Coalition, and an executive with Free Congress, Marshner emerged as a tireless spokesman for the traditional values espoused by the New Right. She is also a relentless and passionate debater. As a result of their varied activities (conducted in a maze of interlocking organizations), Weyrich and his staff had established themselves by the 1980s as the ideological center of social conservatism.

Terry Dolan, the chairman of the National Conservative Political Action Committee (NCPAC), may have been the most controversial New Right leader. Under Dolan, NCPAC devoted its energies to unseating liberals by any possible legal means. Charges against Dolan ranged from slander to blackmail to attacks on his private life. Whatever the substance of the allegations, NCPAC has become a symbol of New Right political successes in mobilizing the politics of resentment. Alan Crawford, a self-styled conservative and author of *Thunder on the Right,* records part of a conversation in which Dolan explained his strategy: the key phrases include, "Let's get rid of the bastards," "Stir up hostilities," and "The shriller you are the better it is to raise money."[4] In a 1977 campaign to defeat the Democratic gubernatorial candidate in Virginia, Dolan's tactics were shrill enough for the Republican candidate to disassociate himself publicly. In the 1986 North Carolina Republican primary contest, Dolan even refused to concede defeat when the conservatives lost but threatened to continue his advertising campaign. North Carolina's New Right Senator, Jesse Helms, was not amused, and some Republicans were quick to blame their candidate's defeat on the divisive primary campaign. However, there is no denying NCPAC's successes. In 1978 alone, it made financial contributions to 200 conservative candidates and provided $440,000 worth of campaign services. In 1980 Dolan's organization reported raising $7.6 million and spending $3.3 million on independent expenditures aimed at unseating liberal Democrats,[5] although by 1986 NCPAC was in serious financial trouble.

In its rise to prominence, NCPAC was an important client of the Richard A. Viguerie Company (RAVCO), a fund-raising and promotion empire that mushroomed in the late seventies. Viguerie learned the business of fund-raising as Marvin Liebman's account executive for YAF, a job that he obtained in 1961 after answering a classified ad in *National Review.* A shy man, Viguerie found it difficult to ask for contributions directly and hit upon the expedient of writing letters. In 1964 he set up his own direct mail firm and built his original list by hand-copying the names of Goldwater supporters. (There does not appear to be a great deal of substance to the allegation that he stole the YAF list.)

Viguerie is a bundle of strange contradictions: a Catholic (like Weyrich) who is closely identified with Christian Fundamentalists; a sincere and committed ideologue (few who know him seem to doubt this) whose company is frequently accused of raking off the lion's share of funds raised for conservative causes; a simple populist who lives in great style in Georgetown. As Viguerie tells his own story, many of his most fateful decisions were made in emotional reaction to some slight, real or imagined. In 1971, for example, he actively sought the Committee to Re-Elect the President (CREEP) account. When he failed, Viguerie began to turn against Nixon and rejected an offer, later that year, to do mailings. He attributed his decision to Nixon's shift to the left: "I decided I wanted no part of Nixon. . . . I realize that Nixon may never have had any deep-rooted belief or goals, except those that furthered his particular personal ambition."

Viguerie and his colleagues have supported—only to reject—a number of Republican politicians: Barry Goldwater, Richard Nixon, John Connally, George Wallace, and Ronald Reagan. Reagan was not the New Right's prime candidate for president—the less conservative but more outspoken John Connally of Texas was the candidate the New Right supported. After Reagan's 1980 victory, it was hoped that the new administration would treat the Heritage Foundation's *Mandate for Leadership* not merely as a blueprint—which it did—but also as a detailed agenda to be followed to the letter. When Reagan proved to be as much politician as ideologue, the cry went up: "Let Reagan be Reagan." And it was not long before Viguerie began to offer alternatives, like Jesse Helms, to the press. At first, the attacks were mostly directed against White House advisers, particularly James Baker, a George Bush Republican accused of blocking conservative appointments. A 1981 Heritage Foundation report on the administration's first year attributed Reagan's mixed performance to "a lack of political sensitivity in the personnel staff." In February of 1982, conservative leaders met with Reagan to discuss their complaints, but by the end of Reagan's first term, New Right leaders were discussing the formation of a third party. For hostile critics, this refusal to "play ball" was a sign of instability in the New Right leadership. In the words of an English chronicler of American conservatism in the Reagan era, Gillian Peele: "The New Right showed an element of self-destructiveness and sectarianism which has perpetually marked much of the thinking and testimony of the Conservative movement."[6]

The sense of betrayal runs deep in New Right circles, and few political leaders have demonstrated an ability to command their loyalty for more than a short period. Conservative politicians, on the other hand, developed doubts about RAVCO's methods. The most frequently heard complaint was that Viguerie's fees practically bankrupted Representative Phil

Crane's presidential bid as well as the campaigns of Iowa Senator Roger Jepsen. In his defense, Viguerie was to point out the enormous start-up costs involved in building a list of contributors, a list that only begins to pay dividends after the fund-raisers had left the scene.

Religious Right

From almost the beginning, the New Right's tactics were controversial. Its image was tarnished in the press, and its coalition sometimes seemed like an unstable assortment of alliances. At least the alliance with Evangelicals proved to be popular among many Americans. By the 1970s politics was hardly a new concern for Evangelical Christians. Much of the support for William Jennings Bryan's populist crusades had been drawn from the Evangelical churches, and the 1950s and 1960s were treated to anticommunist political sermons by the Reverend Carl McIntire and even Billy Graham. Still, the Fundamentalist mainstream, represented by the Bob Jones dynasty in South Carolina, avoided politics and did not hesitate to criticize politically minded preachers.

Jerry Falwell himself used to preach sermons against marching ministers. The key event in waking Falwell and other Fundamentalists from their apolitical slumbers was the 1973 Supreme Court decision on abortion. Most Evangelicals had not given a great deal of thought to what was regarded as a typically Catholic issue, but *Roe* v. *Wade* changed all that by turning a personal moral question into a national political issue. The failure of the main-line churches to oppose the decision and the political escapades of the World Council of Churches contributed to the growing unease of Falwell and others. As Dinesh D'Souza, his recent biographer, puts it: "Abortion politicized, even radicalized Falwell, but as he began to be interested in politics, other issues arose."[7]

In the late 1970s, a number of Christian political groups began to attract attention, particularly the Christian Voice, led by Gary Jarmin, an organization that rated congressmen. The National Christian Action Coalition (NCAC) was another prominent Christian political group. NCAC was particularly engaged in efforts to prevent the IRS from interfering in religious schools. Outside the Evangelical spectrum, Catholics for Christian Political Action focused on the evils of abortion, homosexual rights, and the national defense.

The largest and most conspicuous group on the religious right was the Moral Majority. Established after a May 1979 meeting, its founders included Robert Billups (former director of NCAC), Howard Phillips

(Conservative Caucus), Richard Viguerie, Ed McAteer (Christian Roundtable), Paul Weyrich (Free Congress), and, most significantly, Jerry Falwell of the Thomas Roads Baptist Church in Lynchburg, Virginia. As an obvious sign of Falwell's centrality, the meeting was held in his office—although it was actually Weyrich and McAteer who came up with the name.

In a brief but stormy career, the Moral Majority and its leader were attacked from all sides of the political spectrum. On the left, black leader Julian Bond, George McGovern, and Norman Lear (People for the American Way) pronounced it dangerous and drew comparisons with the Ku Klux Klan and Nazi Germany. On the right, Barry Goldwater suggested it was every American's patriotic duty "to kick Jerry Falwell in the ass." The critical abuse rose to a crescendo when MM began a campaign against network television and raised the possibility of boycotting certain programs. A similar uproar was created in 1985 when a letter-writing campaign put pressure on Southland Corporation (7 Eleven Stores) to remove *Playboy* and *Penthouse* from their magazine racks.

Falwell's response to accusations of bookburning and bigotry was a friendly assertion of democratic pluralism. Old-fashioned Christians and Jews, he repeatedly argued, are entitled to have opinions and to act upon them. "Liberals have been imposing morality on us for the last fifty years,"[8] he declared, and there was nothing wrong in fighting back. On rare occasions, Falwell may have lived down to the stereotype presented in the press. In the beginning, he was not always properly briefed on political questions and had to fall back on scriptural quotations. As time went on, however, he became an adroit politician, affable and deft in handling hecklers and willing to sit down and talk pleasantly with opponents like Ted Kennedy. While it is hard to measure the success of the Moral Majority's efforts, pollster Lou Harris attributes the 1980 election of Ronald Reagan partly to the vote of the awakened Evangelicals. It is an unquestionably large group. Of the 30 million or so estimated Evangelicals, one survey suggests at least a third regularly tune in to religious programming on television.[9] However, estimates of Evangelical strength often include large numbers of Catholic and black voters who do not quite fit the Moral Majority mold. Perhaps this diversity helps to explain why the Christian right has not, by and large, succeeded in realizing its ambitions. Despite a few victories, "the record," as Kenneth Wald suggests, "has been one of failure. Under Ronald Reagan, abortion was still legal, while school prayer was not."[10]

Hostile critics Alan Crawford in *Thunder on the Right* and John Saloma in *Ominous Politics* describe the New Right almost exclusively in the terms of campaign technology and "interlocking directorates": who raises money for whom, who gets appointed to which job through whose influence, and so on—a technique the John Birchers used against the Left. Such an approach deals, however, only with the surface. On a number of important subjects, especially social issues connected with the family and education, the New Right represents a distinctive and fairly consistent position that makes it, in the view of the authors of *Neopolitics,* "the most significant new force in American politics in half a century, and quite possibly the full one hundred years."[11]

Social Issues

Older conservatives were not insensitive to the social and moral questions that agitate the New Right, but the old "fusionist" coalition included a libertarian strain summed up—albeit crudely—in the expression, "You can't legislate morality." Throughout the sixties and seventies, conservatives depicted the federal government as an oppressive agent of moral enforcement through the Civil Rights Act, forced busing, and affirmative action policies. It was inevitably more convenient (and less divisive) to attack existing policies than to offer alternatives. While this alliance against a common enemy helped to keep the "fusionist" coalition together, it also hindered the development of positive vision that went beyond political antistatism and economic freedom.

From the very first, however, the New Right took the offensive on a whole range of controversial issues: sex education, homosexual rights, abortion, school prayer, and the Equal Rights Amendment. At the center of all these issues is the traditional Judeo-Christian conception of the family as a divinely ordained institution. In their view, homosexual behavior is not only unnatural, but contrary to God's will. Marriage exists, especially in Protestant theology, for both companionship and procreation. Homosexuality is, as one Christian Voice appeal for funds put it, part of "a master plan to destroy everything that is good and moral here in America." On this issue, the Religious Right took the lead, and Jerry Falwell went so far as to attack Coors Brewing (a major funding source on the Right) for advertising in a homosexual publication. While Anita Bryant became the symbol of opposition to gay rights, the most serious discussion was provided by Enrique T. Rueda of Paul Weyrich's Free Congress Committee. Rueda cited evidence of government support for the homosexual movement, which he portrayed as a kind of conspiracy against conventional morality. Unlike most attacks on homosexual rights, Rueda's *Homosexual Network* avoided hysterical language and attempted to document its indictment.

When they are accused of imposing their personal morality, Christian activists reply that all laws are a matter of "values." For example, commitments to protection of life and property are not self-evident givens; they are derived from specific cultural and religious traditions. When liberal and Christian traditions collide, the principal question becomes, as Carl Horn expressed in a book title, one of *Whose Values?*: "The conflict is between those who believe that law and public policy derive from religious belief and those who reject such an assumption."[12]

Social conservatives maintain that homosexual rights threaten the family by legitimizing alternative life-styles. For the same reason, an even more serious danger is posed by women's rights. Phyllis Schlafly and her Eagle Forum were successful in preventing what seemed to be the inevitable passage of the Equal Rights Amendment—a victory that caused George Gilder to refer to her as "one of the most effective political leaders ever to emerge in America."[13] Schlafly was herself far from hard line on women's issues. She supported as "benign discrimination" the privileged legal status enjoyed by women in a society that also enforced equal rights under the law.[14] Critics on the Left (and even a few radicals on the Right) complained of the inconsistency in having one's cake and eating it too, but Schlafly was an activist rather than philosopher. Her concern was to defend women, not to draw up a system of political ethics. The efforts of Eagle Forum and of countless state and local anti-ERA organizations caused the Republican party to drop its support in 1980.

There was a single issue campaign even more explosive than stopping ERA or homosexual rights ordinances: abortion. It was an issue that united Evangelical Protestants with traditional Catholics and Orthodox Jews against what columnist Joseph Sobran called "the abortion sect," a materialist worldview that sees man, so critics say, as only "an animal whose destiny is a life of pleasure and comfort."[15] Opposition to abortion ranged from the dignified essays in the *Human Life Review* (edited by J.P. McFadden) to the disciplined and well-coordinated efforts of the National Right to Life Committee all the way to the pugnacious tactics of Joseph Scheidler, who declared open war on abortion clinics.[16] Perhaps the most striking development has been the gradual shift (partly under the influence of the late Francis Schaeffer) from Catholic to Evangelical domination in the movement, although many Evangelicals continue to be more flexible than Catholics (Falwell, for example, considers it a tactical mistake to insist upon a federal law forbidding abortion in every case including rape).

Early in the Reagan years, Senator John East, an Old Right political scientist, held hearings on when life begins, but even a Republican-held Senate was not about to take on a politically explosive topic. By the mid-1980s, however, the subject would not go away. What little traditional Catholic support Geraldine Ferraro brought to the Mondale ticket began to melt away as her "prochoice" position became generally known. Her conflict with Cardinal John O'Connor, archbishop of New York, did little to reassure Catholic voters of her fidelity. Catholics differed little from other Americans who opposed abortion except to save the mother's life or in cases where rape or incest was involved. What had seemed to be the safe, middle course of the seventies—"I'm against abortion personally, but do not wish to impose my views on others"—began to seem, by the eighties, a proabortion argument.

Opposition to ERA, homosexual rights, and abortion was part of what the New Right regarded as a crusade to save the American family. Liberalized divorce laws and a general air of permissiveness had spawned a wide range of "alternate life-styles" that resulted in spiraling rates of divorce, abortion, and adolescent suicide. The tax code, itself, in the view of Allan Carlson, offered massive disincentives for family life. In a series of reports on the family,[17] Carlson argued that Social Security was a scam for breaking up intergenerational family ties, that tax deductions for day care amounted to a subsidy for mothers who neglected their children, and that inflation-eroded personal exemptions constituted an assault on traditional families burdened by the expense of rearing children on a single income.

Carlson was not alone in his concern for family issues. Weyrich's Free Congress established the *Family Protection Report,* a political newsletter on family issues edited by Connaught Marshner and Patrick Fagan. Later Weyrich founded the *Journal of Family and Culture,* edited by Joseph Piccione, as an alternative to more liberal academic publications, particularly the *Journal of Marriage and the Family.* Other prominent participants in the profamily coalition included John Whitehead of the Rutherford Institute and James Dobson, who put out a monthly *Focus on the Family.*

While there was no denying the sincerity of the family's defenders, many of them were severely limited in their approach. Ignoring a mass of evidence from social history, anthropology, and psychology, much of the profamily literature is a series of almost hysterical reactions to events. Some of the writing was fueled by a nostalgic wish to return to the golden age of a simple America. The nuts-and-bolts approach to family policy, characteristic of Weyrich's Free Congress publications, was eminently serviceable in rallying the pro-family forces around specific issues, but it failed to attract and convince serious psychologists, family historians, and sociologists. Allan Carlson, who had connections both with the neoconservatives and the New Right, was a conspicuous exception, but not even he could always avoid the major pitfall of the New Right family coalition: the conviction that the nuclear family was a fragile product of bourgeois society that needed political support from the government. Inevitably, this would invest the government with the power to "protect" the family. This sort of family policy was more typical of European social democrats than American conservatives.

Strange ideas began to emanate from conservative quarters. Both George Gilder and Joseph Piccione came out for government subsidies for children on the model of European social democracy. Previously, conservatives had only sought to reduce government intrusions into private life. The call for government support was uncharacteristic and seemed to call into question the conservative claim that the family was a universal requirement for stable society. If conservatives came to view the family as unable to survive without financial rewards from government, Leftists would have reasons for stepping up their attacks on the family as a "patriarchal" institution.

This paradox becomes clear in discussions of parents' rights. Much of the debate on the subject is concerned with a minor's right to an abortion, the parents' role in sex and values education, and child-abuse legislation. Until the twentieth century, families were generally responsible for the moral instruction (and behavior) of minor children. Increasingly, however, schools and social work agencies have come to define what is in the children's interests.

By the late 1970s, the idea of children's rights began to surface. Sex education, contraception, religious and racial tolerance, and mental health began to be seen as human rights to be guaranteed by law. The process was encouraged by the United Nation's International Year of the Child and a similar program in the United States. Decent treatment for children seemed to be an unimpeachable idea to many people, but conservatives viewed it as one more stage in the state's usurpation of family responsibilities. In fact, much of the proposed child protection legislation (especially child-abuse laws) bypassed the ordinary civil rights of accused persons and acted against parents on the presumption of guilt.

There is an obvious conservative strategy illustrated in the writings of Mary Pride:[18] This is to challenge the child-abuse statistics and to document the sufferings of innocent parents in the grip of a coercive legal system. The Leftist Christopher Lasch, in his book *Haven in a Heartless World,* has also deplored the therapeutic state that has grown at the expense of families. Here was a rare chance for a Left/Right antigovernment consensus.

But many conservatives go farther. Not content with attempting to undo the misuse of government power, many argue that such power must be used to defend and build up the power of the family. John W. Whitehead of the Rutherford Institute bases such an argument on the dubious claim (derived from Alvin Toffler!) that the fragile family structure is breaking down.[19] Fears of widespread family dissolution serve as a pretext for activists on the Right and social workers on the Left to uphold governments' claims to be the ultimate authority on social and ethical questions. In the end, at least some pro-family arguments may have the effect of diminishing family autonomy.

The more sensible and intelligent profamily activists are not unaware of the tension between their resentment of big government and their desire to use that same government to buttress the family. Until now, Connaught Marshner explains the government has been working to undermine the family, but a New Right State could do a number of useful things: exclude alternative living arrangements from the legal definition of family, give financial protection to mothers in need, make divorce more difficult, and recognize the historic rights of parents in the education of their children.

The New Right's education campaign has been aimed primarily at questions of ethics and religion. At stake is the right of schools to decide on curriculum as against the right of parents to determine what sort of moral and religious values their children will be taught. The focus of much of the criticism has been on sex education and values clarification (what is sometimes called ethical reasoning). In 1984 the Department of Education held hearings on the Protection of Pupils Rights Amendment. Edited (and widely distributed) by Phyllis Schlafly,[20] the testimony was used to demonstrate the immorality and underhanded techniques of values-education classes. What Evangelicals called "secular humanism" was being taught, while references to God and religion were being excluded from textbooks and curricula. In a study supported by the Department of Education, Paul Vitz made a detailed examination of social studies textbooks and found virtually no mention of such momentous religious events as the Great Awakening.[21] Elementary school reading books do inculcate values, Vitz concluded: They are against patriotism and business but support feminism, and "serious Judeo-Christian religious motivation" is featured nowhere.[22]

Since the Scopes trial in the 1920s, education has been a battleground between the forces of academic liberalism and middle-American populism. Issues like busing in South Boston or textbooks in West Virginia and Tennessee have been able to galvanize support for a New Right agenda. Reagan's head of the U.S. Department of Education, William Bennett, defused some of the growing antagonism, but the hostility runs too deep for any rhetorical solutions. By the 1980s New Right and religious activists were on the offensive, demanding full support for their views. *Washington Times* columnist John Lofton, for example, in interviewing Secretary Bennett, refused to be placated by general reassurances. What Lofton and others insist on is (1) the primacy of revelation and (2) the unconditional right of parents to determine what their children are taught. Bennett, on the other hand, was willing to grant only a qualified support for the importance of religion and the need for parental involvement. After Reagan, education may well turn out to be the most explosive item on the New Right agenda.

While the New Right is most prominently identified with social issues, it has not shied away from other political questions, particularly foreign policy. Jerry Falwell and Pat Robertson regularly made statements on South Africa, the Soviet occupation of Afghanistan, and Nicaragua. It was conventional politics that brought into prominence Viguerie, Weyrich, and Phillips, all of whom appeared opposed to President Carter's 1977 proposal to democratize political campaigns.[23] Ironically, several aspects of Carter's proposal, for example, his plan to abolish the electoral college, were populist in nature and deserved New Right support.

On foreign policy, the New Right organizations worked against the Panama Canal treaties, arms limitation agreements, and economic sanctions against South Africa. On the other hand, they supported aid to "freedom fighters" in Nicaragua, Afghanistan, and Angola. The Angolan rebel Jonas Savimbi became a favorite cause; and an article appeared under his name in the Heritage Foundation's *Policy Review*. Howard Phillips was particularly active in demanding that U.S. companies pull out of Soviet-dominated Angola—a conservative version of "disinvestment."[24]

Agenda or Social Philosophy?

The New Right/Religious Right has staked out positions on a broad array of subjects. They are against abortion, gun control, sex education,

ERA, dealings with Communist regimes, and high taxes; while they favor censorship, restoration of religious values, support for anticommunist guerrilla movements, and self-determination for states and municipalities. Hostile critics see this coalition of single issues either as the opportunism of fund-raisers or the symptoms of a reactionary backlash. One question that is rarely asked is whether or not the New Right possesses anything like a positive vision of social life that could be called a political philosophy. The answer may be no and yes: No, if we are looking for a systematic exposition of first principles of the type offered by Thomas Hobbes or Karl Marx, but yes, if we mean an implicit set of assumptions that can be stated systematically.

Few New Right representatives would express interest in political philosophy. Viguerie, on his own account, was a mediocre student in mediocre schools. Weyrich and Phillips, by contrast, are intellectually quick but prefer to avoid most first-principle discussions. The reason for this is neither lack of conviction nor educational deficiency. Pat Robertson of Christian Broadcasting Network is among the best-educated political figures in the United States, but he shares with other Fundamentalists a certain suspicion of abstract analysis. When solid academics join forces with the New Right, they almost invariably choose to work on the everyday level of policy questions. Charles Moser, for example, is a distinguished scholar in Slavic studies who has worked closely with Weyrich's Free Congress Committee; his work for them, however, is unrelated to his scholarship in Bulgarian and Russian literature.

One effort was made to work out a New Right philosophy in a volume of essays edited by Robert W. Whitaker entitled *The New Right Papers*.[25] Whitaker himself was an eccentric populist and author of *A Plague on Both Your Houses,* a provocative work predicting the overthrow of the liberal elite of *both* political parties. *The New Right Papers* included statements from the leadership—Viguerie and Weyrich—as well as contributions from sympathetic members of the Old Right like William Rusher and Jeffrey Hart of *National Review.* However, the three essays that drew the most fire from reviewers were made by three relatively unknown scholars, all with University of North Carolina Ph.D.'s. Their essays were controversial, precisely because they attempted to articulate a set of New Right political principles that combined a populist/Jacksonian defense of the common man with the respect for tradition and order characteristic of the Old Right.

The emphasis was strongly on what the writers regarded as the authentic republican tradition of the American people. "Liberty," as historian Clyde Wilson argued, "was a by-product of membership in good standing of a free community, not a grant from government." Wilson opposed the false democracy of managed elections and rejected what he called the "imperialism" of a government that ruled in its own interest: "The New Right, it seems to me, may best be understood as a largely spontaneous and as-yet-imperfectly-articulated defense of the American community (or rather communities, for there are several) against the inroads of imperialism." Wilson rejected equally the exaltation of the state and the celebration of individual freedom, while locating the political center in family and community. The American system of civic responsibility, he insisted, was not derived from abstract proclamations of rights. It was a living inheritance bequeathed by European (especially British) and American ancestors. It was real and rooted but not universal.[26]

Another essay, "Old Rights and the New Left," was even more explicit in rejecting both the individualist tradition of natural rights and the statism that inevitably ensued.[27] In defense of "the Southern tradition" in politics, the author rejected not only natural rights but any ideology of freedom that eroded family and community: "The destruction of the family began long ago in the apparently innocent decision of state and local governments to provide for schools. Public education . . . has turned out to be the principal weapon used by the enemies of the family." Not only government provoked the Southern apologist's fire; big business capitalists were held just as accountable for teaching equal opportunity at the expense of family integrity and for "turning a blind, libertarian eye" to the moral questions of divorce and pornography. Free enterprise was a positive good, but, as Clyde Wilson warned, only as "part of the genius of the American people." It was "not an absolute"; he insisted: "It is a means, not an end. New Rightists, including those who devote their lives productively to free enterprise, do not intend to establish a religion of the dollar bill."[28] The Southern apologist agreed. Free enterprise was "the best of all economic systems" but certainly not "a way of life":

Our social vision, it must be argued, is not limited to a choice between economic theories of political life—capitalism and socialism—both reflexes of the same degraded, aluminum coin, both sound as the paper dollar.

. . . The hardest tasks for conservatives will be to convince our capitalist allies that the common rights of humanity, as embodied in the family, and our civil rights as Englishmen and Americans take precedence over our desire for profits and productivity.[29]

The New Right's hostility to sex education, the ERA, forced busing, and no-fault divorce might be plausibly explained as a rejection of the liberal natural rights philosophy that had dominated political discourse since John Locke. The values of ordinary Americans were to be taken seriously not so much because they were reactionary or because as individuals they possessed rights. It was rather that families, communities, and regions were by nature suited to carry out certain functions that were spelled out in the doctrine of natural law. In the natural law tradition of Aristotle, Cicero, and medieval Catholicism, God had inscribed his will in the heart, or as we now say, the instincts of the human species. Mothers did not have to be told to take care of children or forgo sexual relations with male offspring, since they were naturally so predisposed. What instinct failed to inculcate, the faculty of right reason would. Without really employing the language of natural law, the New Right agenda took much of it for granted.

All that was lacking to this potent combination of reactionary political theory with single issues voting blocks was a practical strategy for taking power. Such a plan was worked out by Kevin Phillips, William Rusher, and perhaps most interestingly by Samuel T. Francis in his contribution to *The New Right Papers*. Borrowing the term "Middle American Radicals" (MARS) from Donald Warren's *The Radical Center: Middle America and the Politics of Alienation,* Francis integrated the idea into the conceptual framework of Italian political theory (i.e., Mosca and Pareto) and James Burnham's *The Managerial Revolution.* The task, as Francis saw it, was "to dismantle or radically reform the managerial appetites of social control" and to strive for "the localization, privatization, and decentralization of the managerial apparatus of power."[30]

There were foreign policy implications to this thesis. Francis appealed to American "nationalism." From the perspective of Middle American entrepreneurs, "the military and economic preeminence of the United States" would become the primary objectives. A new mercantilism was proposed that would provide "some measure of protection for domestic producers." New Right politicians would win support by standing up for American interests against "Third World arrogance, aggression, and barbarianism." A president who learned to apply such a strategy might practice an American "Caesarism" and dismantle the managerial apparatus.[31]

Populists or Conservatives?

By the beginning of 1984, Richard Viguerie and his friends were already discussing the formation of a populist party alternative to both the Democrats and Republicans—a shift predicted by Robert Whitaker several years earlier. They were against big government, big labor, and most significantly, big business. Viguerie advanced these populist themes in his book *The Establishment vs. the People.* While a reviewer in *Fortune* was both amused and alarmed,[32] the New Right populists were in serious danger of alienating mainstream Republicans and of losing the support of conservative businessmen.

Viguerie proclaimed his populist creed in the bastion of Old Right/pro-business conservatism, *National Review.* In "A Populist and Proud of It"[33] he claimed both Jefferson and William F. Buckley as precursors for "opposition to the elitists." His arguments did little to reassure moderate Republicans in Virginia, who overwhelmingly rejected Viguerie's bid for the Republican nomination for lieutenant governor. Voters may have short memories, but stalwart Republicans might still remember Viguerie's tepid support for Reagan and his willingness to work for conservative Democrats. The campaign cost Viguerie months of time and effort that could have been directed to his business. It also cost about a half million dollars of his own money.

Although Viguerie was often accused of avarice and unscrupulous business practices, it was ironically his idealism and generosity that brought his empire to the brink of ruin in 1985. His insufficient loyalty to the Republican party helped to sour his primary fight and his willingness to extend credit to financially dubious causes resulted in a cash crunch that forced him to sell *Conservative Digest,* his main publication, and to lay off most of his work force. The whole technique of direct mail fund-raising began to be called into question as response rates and average contributions went down. Not just RAVCO, but also NCPAC and even Weyrich's political action committee were in serious danger. By early 1986, however, Viguerie was back in business with new clients and a less optimistic business strategy.[34]

Viguerie's populist rhetoric alarmed the Republican mainstream at the same time that Paul Weyrich was attempting to build bridges to the Republican Center and even to the Democratic Left. Late in 1985, Senator Robert Dole agreed to host a $250-a-plate dinner for Weyrich. (Dole also hired conservative Donald Devine to run "Campaign America.") In building coalitions, the object is either to articulate a set of common principles or at least to identify a common enemy. The New Right had already exploited the negative campaign attack. Perhaps the time had come for a more positive method.

By 1986 Weyrich was promoting what he called "cultural conservatism" and employing the talents of William S. Lind.[35] While Lind and

Weyrich seem to oppose the rationalist skepticism of the French Enlight-
enment, Lind, at least, refuses to embrace either revelation or natural
law as the basis for cultural conservatism. Lind's creed endorses "Western Judeo-Christian values" but "doesn't require anyone to believe traditional values are true *absolutely,* that they derive from God, from
natural law, or from some other source outside secular human experience." He goes on to add: "Politically, it does not matter whether an
individual sees traditional values as absolutely true or only functionally
true. Either belief leads to the same political actions, actions intended to
reaffirm and reinforce those values, to lead the nation and the government to advocate them, and to make them once again define the political
center. . . ."

Perhaps cultural conservatism will prove to be a rallying cry for a re-
vived conservative movement that embraces Old Right intellectuals,
New Right activists, neoconservative policy analysts, and liberals concerned with civility and serious literature. Nonetheless, obstacles to this
alliance do remain.

In the first place, few New Rightists have displayed much interest in
literature, the arts, or philosophy. It is all very well to talk of traditions
and values, but problems arise over details. Are Rousseau and Hume
both skeptics, part of the preferred tradition? What of the pagan classics
that many Evangelical Christians object to? What will cultural conservatism say on the subject of modern art?

Of far greater seriousness is a problem that Lind has deliberately built
into his creed: neutrality on the subject of divine will and natural law.
While it is possible to argue that Fundamentalist Christians and atheist
sociobiologists possess a common view of human nature, it is harder to
broaden that agreement to include those who think the family only *happens* to be functionally important. It is hard to imagine the Religious Right
fighting under the same flag with well-intentioned secular humanists.

Chester Finn, assistant secretary of education, has attempted to take
up the challenge of filling in the blanks of cultural conservatism. In an
American Spectator essay, Finn listed ten tenets and the strategies that
flow from them. The first is respect for Western civilization and the
Judeo-Christian tradition, which requires us to redesign school curricula
to include "cultural literacy." Other tenets include recognizing the importance of beliefs, sanctity of the individual, democracy, the safety and
liberty of individuals, a patriotic mythology, etc.[36]

There are two main problems with Finn's recommendations: by themselves, they are neither cultural nor conservative. By employing the

usual language of rights ("No one may invade another's rights"), Finn explicitly endorses a political philosophy alien to most conservative thought; by setting up democracy as the ideal, he loads the dice both against the authoritarian and the libertarian strains of American conservatism, and by erecting a national pantheon and patriotic calendar ("Independence Day, Memorial Day, Martin Luther King's birthday, Easter"), he is running the same risks as the social architects of the Eisenhower years. A vital culture cannot be designed by federal bureaucrats or created by popular magazines, and it may be too much to hope that Middle American Christians will both celebrate Easter and learn to venerate the memory of Dr. King.

There is more than a little presumption in any attempt to define a culture. Magisterial literary figures like Samuel Johnson, Matthew Arnold, and T.S. Eliot command our respect in such matters, precisely because they had already established themselves as important writers before they began laying down the law. In the United States of the 1980s, there was no Arnold or Eliot in a position to pronounce an American culture. Indeed, no great poet or novelist was willing to identify himself as a conservative, although Walker Percy, the Catholic novelist, did admit to voting for Reagan.

It is the religious conservatives who have the strongest convictions, the clearest worldview, and the largest number of votes (as well as the most vocal enemies). As this book comes to press, the most significant event for the New Right is clearly the candidacy of Pat Robertson for the presidential nomination of the Republican party.

Vociferously opposed by People for the American Way, Robertson points to his credentials as a lawyer and his business success in building up the Christian Broadcasting Network into a powerful communications empire. Whether a Pentecostal broadcaster can convert a viewing audience into a political movement remains to be seen. If Robertson should succeed in making a real race for the nomination (nomination, even without election, would be a genuine miracle), he will have radically shifted the base of the Republican coalition.

Chapter Six

Postscript: Reagan and Beyond

Nineteen eighty was the *anno domini* of American conservatism. Just as the activities of Senator McCarthy were instrumental in creating a conservative movement, Ronald Reagan's election and administration redefined the movement, decided its priorities, and finally condemned some of its principles and causes to outer darkness.

The president was known, even in his days as the "ultraconservative" governor of California, as a coalition builder. From the very beginning of his first administration, Reagan chose to concentrate on issues that united conservatives: rebuilding the American economy and containing the spread of communism. The president did, on occasion, find time for New Right social issues. More than once he put on record his opposition to abortion, and his second attorney general, Edwin Meese, chaired a controversial commission to explore the relationship between pornography and crime. A similar effort on family policy was directed by assistant secretary of education Gary Bauer. However, the Bauer Commission generated little support for the moderate proposal to increase the personal exemption for children on federal income taxes.

In general, Reagan's New Right initiatives were regarded as window dressing for a less than fully conservative administration. If populist conservatives were less than ecstatic, some survivors of the Old Right were swiftly and permanently disenchanted with the new president. One usually unspoken assumption of the Old Right was a defense of European and American civilizations against the Third World. Colonial regimes in

Africa were to be defended, not merely because they worked better than the Marxist military regimes that replaced them but because they were symbols of European man's manifest destiny.

Most of those who held such views would have resented the imputation of racist motives. But whatever the motive, there was no denying conservative support for colonial regimes. Reagan as president did little or nothing to accommodate the national pride of the Old Right and of Southern conservatives. Under his administration, a national holiday was declared in celebration of Dr. Martin Luther King, Jr., and South Africa became the target of economic sanctions, and—perhaps most seriously—next to nothing was done to seal off the Mexican border, much less to repatriate the large numbers of illegal aliens from Central and South America.

For most conservatives who spoke out on these issues—senators Helms and East, as well as Old Right intellectuals like M.E. Bradford, Samuel T. Francis, and *National Review* senior editor Chilton Williamson, Jr.—the issue was not one of race but of civilization. Conservatism usually implies the defense of something, and in the eyes of many traditionalists, the failure to "take up the white man's burden," which had spelled the doom of the British Empire, would soon destroy an America that turned its back on allies like South Africa and refused to recognize that the basically European stock and traditions on which the United States was built was incompatible with the hordes of non-European illegal immigrants.

The Old Right mentality was as much instinct or taste as a set of commitments, and the truest of proverbs remains *de gustibus non disputandum est.* One cannot conduct an argument on questions of taste. Indeed, the unraveling of the conservative alliance was related to differences in temperament and taste. Much of the Old Right's outlook was determined by an inchoate patriotism, a sentimental affection for what remained of the old America. Washington Irving, Henry Adams, the Southern Agrarians, and Russell Kirk all shared this dim sense of *pietas* both to America and to its European antecedents. As Peter and Brigitte Berger suggested in a *Commentary* article (October 1986), "Our Conservatism and Theirs," traditionalists were fond of looking back to the Middle Ages (if they were Catholic), the seventeenth century (if, like T.S. Eliot, they were Anglicans), the early nineteenth century (if they were Southerners), or the late nineteenth century (if they were libertarian capitalists). While the Bergers' classification is a commonplace of conservative conversation (and far from applicable to most living and breathing conservatives), it is still useful as an index to stylistic preference.

By their own account, the Bergers themselves were German Lutherans whose experience of the United States was concentrated on New York and the Northeast. Geography, they suggest, is as telling as a chronological frame of reference in determining one's conservative affiliation: traditionalists live almost everywhere but New York, while neoconservatives are at home almost nowhere else. From the perspective of the urban Northeast, America is a society of immigrants held together by an ideology of democratic capitalism, but from the perspective of the South and the nonurban Midwest, one is most impressed by the historical saga of flesh-and-blood men and women building, generation by generation, a community on the frontier. The Constitution, the Bill of Rights, and democratic capitalism would be viewed merely as artifacts of the American experience: they were made by Americans; they did not make America.

The prospects for an enduring conservative coalition that is composed of such disparate elements depend on a number of factors. One is the willingness of all parties to play fair and treat each other with civility; another is the seriousness of the threat by "the common enemy"; a third is the degree to which there is a serious conversation between the various groups as well as a willingness to engage in an open discussion of first principles.

Fair Play

All three representative groups have voiced complaints about the tactics and behavior of their allies. Neoconservatives were quick to point out the reactionary tendencies of both Old Right and New Right conservatives. There is no doubt that more than a few highly esteemed conservative idols expressed sentiments that might be regarded as anti-Semitic. Hilaire Belloc and G.K. Chesterton, two favorite writers for Catholic conservatives, believed that Jews would not or could not become loyal English citizens. Of course, in fairness, it should be pointed out that Chesterton and Belloc were not racists, but critical of Jews for political reasons.

T.S. Eliot is similarly accused of anti-Semitism, largely on the strength of his lectures, *After Strange Gods,* and his friendship with Ezra Pound. In Eliot's case, however, it seems clear that he was far more "pro-Christian" than he was anti anything. The same defense, perhaps, cannot be made of American journalists like Albert Jay Nock and H.L. Mencken, and there was at least vestigial anti-Semitism among some conservatives of the fifties, if not among their intellectual leaders. One of the founders of the John Birch Society, Revilo P. Oliver, recounts that while they agreed to refer to the international Communist Conspiracy, everyone would know what that meant."[1]

Although Oliver was an eccentric who may not have spoken for more than a handful in the Society (which was only a fringe group on the Right), there were legitimate reasons for concern among Jewish neoconservatives. Ethnic and religious prejudices are a probably ineradicable part of human nature, and it is the least cosmopolitan elements of a society (the heartland constituency of conservatism) that is most susceptible.

But ethnic prejudice is not confined to Middle America. In some instances, anti-anti-Semitism may become as violent as the passion it seeks to suppress. Criticism of Israel by the 1980s was becoming sufficient grounds for branding a writer as an anti-Semite. On the other hand, as neoconservatives are all too well aware, anti-Semitism is increasingly a disease of the Far Left, and not of the Christian Right. Diatribes against Israel or against Jewish influence are far more likely to be found in the pages of *The Nation*[2] than in those of *Human Events*. In the context of the 1980s, however, columnist Joseph Sobran's naive attacks on the "Israel lobby," even if they had a grain of truth, were far from helpful in maintaining a conservative coalition.

Open Discussion

While renewed fears of bigotry on the Right served to poison the spirit of amity that had developed in the 1970s, there was a more serious effect. The impulse to egalitarianism, always strong in the United States, derived added strength from the threat of anti-Semitism. Throughout the Reagan years, libertarians, business-oriented Republicans, and neoconservatives insisted that the American Way rested on the twin pillars of freedom and equal opportunity. Michael Novak's 1982 book, *The Spirit of Democratic Capitalism,* exemplified a trend that the Bergers were to proclaim as the only path to human well-being: "Given the realities of the contemporary world, we are in favor of maintaining the major existing institutions of American society. These institutions are, roughly, contained in the phrase 'democratic capitalism.'" In the Bergers' view, traditionalists are "under an illusion" in thinking that they can hold on to the certitude of "cherished traditions," because every traditionalist chooses his own tradition. Paradoxically, then, freedom of choice would become the only basis for traditionalism.

If this argument were taken seriously, it would exclude the entire traditionalist wing of the conservative movement—and possibly the existence of any community-based moral custom. A leading Southern traditionalist, M.E. Bradford, gave a response, unintentionally, in the course of a speech to the Heritage Foundation on 21 October 1986. In exploring the conservative strain in the American experience, Bradford restated the old federal principle of limited government: "All of our social myths presupposed some version of the corporate life—that man is a social being, fulfilled only in the natural associations built upon common experience, upon the ties of blood and friendship. . . ." The passion for equality, Bradford argues, "threatens to swallow up our reverence for law, responsible character, moral principle, and inherited prescription."

In his conclusion, Bradford spelled out the consequences of adopting democratic egalitarianism as a conservative credo:

All of us know that it is "disreputable" and explosive, even in a Washington governed by Ronald Reagan, to complain of egalitarianism, except for the strictly economic variety, which we manage to resist. However, if we continue to commit ourselves to this confusion, not one component of that rich patrimony of which I have spoken can survive. For equality of condition qua equality of opportunity will fill in all the valleys and pull down the hills—create a power which in the name of all good purposes will be enabled in all cases whatsoever to do with us as it will. Those who wish to follow that broad road to Zion (or perdition) may do so. There is a safety and an accommodation with the powers in such choices. You will not be called "insensitive" or "racist" or "cruel." Your position will be respectable (as the enemy defines respectability), but not conservative, as any of our fathers would have understood the word. For we can only do as the Left does if we begin all of our deliberations concerning practice and policy with its fundamental premise in the place of our own.

Neither Bradford nor the Bergers qualify as extremists. To some extent, Bradford's insistence on a robust appreciation of the American heritage was shared not only by Southern conservatives but also by many outside the conservative movement and outside the South. On the other hand, it would be pointless to pretend that the Bergers were latecomers, recent converts to a conservative worldview. Bradford's defense of natural associations would be more than welcome to Peter Berger, the sociologist who has often celebrated such "mediating structures" as the family and the church. If either group succeeds in reading the other out of the party or in closing off discussion on points of fundamental principle, the American conservative movement may be safely consigned to the same dustbin that holds the ashes of the Know-Nothing party.

It is difficult to see how a single principle of economic freedom, the Nicene Creed, or equal opportunity could bind together either a living political coalition or a vital intellectual movement. There are two obvious kinds of dead conservatisms. The first, which alarms the proponents of democratic capitalism, is an excessive piety to the past. A few Jacobites still toast the "King over the water," more than a hundred years after the death of the last Stuart claimant to the English throne; some Southerners still lament the disappearance of the Confederacy; and there are Hapsburg supporters, Bourbon legitimists, and at least one American conservative who would kneel in the presence of a Palaeologus heir to the throne of Constantinople. Such antique loyalties may be harmless diversions, but they can also be viewed, especially by politicians, as a distraction from the serious business of the here-and-now. Nostalgia is sometimes a poisonous sentiment, as Edward A. Robinson's Miniver Cheevy learned to his sorrow. Too much in love with old books or Burke's vision of chivalrous Europe:

> Miniver Cheevy, born too late,
> Scratched his head and kept on thinking;
> Miniver coughed, and called it fate,
> And kept on drinking.

But if nostalgic traditionalism threatens to become as dead as faith without works, the same is still more true of any form of "presentism." Russell Kirk might strike Leftists as a visitor from another time, but Kirk's conservative vision encompasses centuries, indeed millennia. Those who turn their backs on tradition and look only to the present and near future reject what G.K. Chesterton called "the democracy of the dead." "Tradition," he insisted in "The Ethics of Elfland," "refuses to submit to the small and arrogant oligarchy of those who merely happen to be walking about. All democrats object to men being disqualified by the accident of birth; tradition objects to their being disqualified by the accident of death."

The great promise held out by the conservatism of the 1970s was not the practical fusionism of the 1960s—or periodic updatings of Meyer's yoking of tradition and capitalism. The conservative promise of the seventies was an attempt to unite a concern for social and political health with the ethical and social traditions of the civilized West. If Irving Kristol could give only two cheers for capitalism, that was as much as many traditionalists were able to give. The heart of the new coalition lay precisely in the suspicion that slogans like democracy and free enterprise did not constitute the whole duty of man. Many of the neoconservatives possessed a distinct advantage in coming from the Left: they had learned early on that social justice could not be reduced to mere individual utility. Seeking to demonstrate their bona fides, many of them ran the risk of being "more Catholic than the pope" in questions of national defense and free enterprise.

The principal liability of political sloganeering consists not so much in the antagonisms it arouses as in the effect it has on serious discussion. If every society takes its tone and character from its elite class—as Gaetano Mosca and Antonio Gramsci both argued—it is equally true that ideological movements will not rise above the level of discussion maintained by their intellectual leadership. Common sense dictates that some avenues are closed to conservatives, for example, nationalization of industries and the extirpation of religion, but on other topics humility is said to be the begining of wisdom.

The search for orthodoxy, which did so much to isolate conservative intellectuals in the 1960s, continued in new forms into the 1980s. In many ways, capitalism was an inappropriate bulwark of conservative thought. There is no reason why conservatives should refuse to acknowledge the conflict between an unfettered marketplace and certain social institutions, particularly the family. In an important essay in *Tikkun,* "What's Wrong With the Right?," Christopher Lasch pointed out that the old family wage system has collapsed, practically compelling young mothers to seek employment outside the home, but on this matter, conservatives, by remaining silent, exhibited their "intellectual debility."

Common Enemies

The vehement leftist attacks on neoconservatives, made by journalists like Michael Kinsley of the *New Republic,* Christopher Hitchens of the *Nation,* and Sidney Blumenthal of the *Washington Post,* would seem only to have strengthened the converts' determination to remain on the Right. Some early allies, like Daniel Bell and Seymour Martin Lipset, grew to disdain the label; however, even they showed little sign of drifting back to the committed Left. What is more likely is that many scholars formerly on the Left will remain in a continued state of political disenchantment.

The populist New Right also faced some temptation to veer leftward in a search for allies against big business. Much of the populist program at the turn of the century was explicitly socialist and attracted many radicals. But the American Left of the 1980s was a far cry from 1900. New Right supporters may never learn to endure the Left's hostility to religion and American traditions. Here and there a few old pro-American Leftists like Erwin Knoll of the *Progressive* continued to offer a radical/populist critique of American institutions, but they were the rare exception.

The problem facing conservatives in the years after Reagan grow out of the very coalition that he had helped to assemble: how to keep the blue-collar supporters of the New Right in an alliance with a more intellectual conservative movement dominated by (predominantly) Catholic Old Rightists and (predominantly) Jewish neoconservatives. One of the architects of the populist/conservative strategy, Kevin Phillips, became convinced by the early seventies that the alliance was doomed to fail. In his analysis of *Post–Conservative America*[3] Phillips argued that the Republican party would lose the populist support that Richard Nixon and Ronald Reagan had managed to attract. This did not have to mean the destruction of the conservative/populist cause. In hard political terms, Phillips suggested that the New Right would be "pretty much a spent force by the end of the 1980s," if only because it would have succeeded in putting its "moral and religious agenda" into the mainstream of political debate. In any event, Phillips insists, it was the populist cause that put Reagan into the White House, and it would be populists who will defect first from the coalition.

Two factors make this defection likely, in our view. First, the loss of credibility on the part of New Right leaders and fund-raisers. Middle American radicals are less easily led than any other voting block, and by 1985 they were already showing signs of disaffection. Second, the Democrats were already moving to convert the family issue into a part of the welfare and compassion rhetoric they had used successfully since the 1930s.[4] Whatever else it may have meant, the elections of 1986, which restored control of the Senate to the Democrats, did not constitute a ringing endorsement of the GOP.

A Four-sided Commonwealth

While most commentators continued to discuss American politics in terms of a Left/Right dichotomy, a more complex scheme—circulated among libertarians by the Cato Institute—began to seem more appropriate: liberal, libertarian, conservative, populist.

The task of any 1980s coalition was to keep at least two of these elements more or less in harmony. Reagan's electoral success lay in combining conservative strength with support from blue-collar populists and "Yuppies" with a libertarian attitude in social and economic matters.[5] To the extent that Evangelical Christians like Pat Robertson increase their influence in the Republican party, affluent urban professionals will be driven to seek alternatives. Republicans in the late eighties will have to decide the character of their party; conservatives will have to decide where to place their allegiance—in a world of shifting political coalitions. It is far from certain that American conservatism can survive in its present state into the 1990s. It is also unclear whether the Republican party will continue to accommodate conservatives, however well they may resolve their own disputes.

The political undoing of conservatives may come not from internal dissension, but from the rise of the Yuppie influence within the Republican party. A Republican party that seeks to woo this group through a combination of socially liberal and selectively libertarian fiscal policies will be effectively driving out conservatives. Even the neoconservatives may feel uncomfortable in a party that caters to gays and ceases to defend the nuclear family.

If conservatives were to abandon the GOP, it would not be to join the Democratic party. This could only happen if the Democrats did something even less likely, withdraw from their left-of-center base to pursue intellectuals and hypothetical constituencies on the Right. Another possibility remains: forming a third party that represents conservative principles. Yet it is doubtful that such a third party would carry substantial numbers of voters in a society with a strong two-party system. One may be justified in wondering whether old conservatives, New Rightists, and neoconservatives could even agree on a third-party candidate, let alone elect him.

Conservatism as a Social Movement

The prospects of electoral success for the conservative movement depend, in part, on the ability of the various groups to attract a mass base that aims at significant structural changes in American government and society. While we have in this study concentrated on the theory and practice of intellectuals and activists, it is only as a social movement that postwar conservatism can have a real impact on everyday life.

The three main groups of 1980s conservatives are clearly divided on this question. While the New Right leaders have seen their work solely in terms of creating a mass-based social movement, the neoconservatives have, in effect, rejected any thought of a popular following and aim their efforts exclusively at disaffected members of the social and intellectual elites. The Old Right continues to be what it has always been, a series of negotiated truces between intellectuals (both traditionalist and capitalist) and a popular following of anticommunists, social conservatives, and traditionalist Catholics.

In a review of Sidney Blumenthal's *The Rise of The Counter-Establishment* (published in the *New Republic*), Eugene Genovese criticizes Blumenthal for his failure to distinguish between neoconservatives and the Old Right. The waning of neoconservative influence that Blumenthal predicts need not result, says Genovese, in a political and cultural gain to the Left. It may in fact "bring forward a much harder and more radical right, with serious political prospects." Recruiting heavily from the South, this resurgent Right has already incorporated elements of the Southern Agrarian tradition: "Today with the work of M.E. Bradford, it has established a political base of indeterminate but clearly not trivial proportions." Moreover, "the Northern contingent has always had a strong dose of high Romanism, but in addition to Stephen Tonsor and other Catholics, it has included Russell Kirk, and such younger scholars as Paul Gottfried. Together, the traditionalists and the Straussians, whose influence in the universities remains limited but noteworthy, constitute an impressive array of educators, many of whom are scholars and teachers of a high order."[6] Genovese attributes to the reinvigorated Old Right a strategic sense related to its dark but realistic view of human nature.

Several aspects of Genovese's analysis are hard to accept. Does the Old Right have more "serious political prospects" than the neoconservatives? Unless Genovese or someone else outlines a plausible sequence of events by which Old Rightists can take over the government and major educational institutions, his statement must be treated as purely conjectural. Nor can one dispense with the problem of proof by conjuring up an Old Right political base in the South "of indeterminate but clearly not trivial proportions." Genovese seriously misreads the *Southern Partisan* as a significant force. Started by Old Right Southern scholars, it rapidly passed into the control of Republican party operatives. Without intellectual credibility, the *Partisan* has not created a mass following. Even if its subscription list were combined with *Modern Age,* the number is far smaller than the readership of either *Commentary* or the *New Republic.*

Genovese is correct on one essential point: of all groups today identified as conservative, the Old Right can most accurately be described as a social movement. Though certainly not the best financed or most publicized group on the Right, it is nonetheless the only one that embodies three crucial characteristics of a social movement: it can claim a popular base (however sectionalized it may be); an intellectual elite; and a commitment to far-reaching political reforms. Though weakened by steady defections to other camps, the Old Right has preserved its identity as a social movement since the early 1960s. The emergence of state conservative parties and the Goldwater campaign helped create a conservative constituency among Southern white and, to a lesser extent, among Northern ethnic voters. The same voters, as Kevin Phillips has shown, remained critical for Republican presidential victories afterwards, including the Reagan victories in 1980 and 1984. It would be an exaggeration to identify these voting groups exclusively with the Old Right because of the inroads among them that Old Rightists made in the 1960s. Yet the Old Right continues to possess a cadre of Washington supporters comprising senators, congressmen, and congressional aides particularly from the South and Southwest. When M.E. Bradford launched his bid for the NEH directorship, he obtained the active and often impetuous support of more than twenty senators and sixty congressmen. Unlike William Bennett, his eventually successful neoconservative rival, Bradford, a former Democratic county chairman in Texas, pursued a career in politics as well as in academic life. His close friend, John East, junior senator from North Carolina, moved in the opposite direction. A prominent theorist of the Old Right and a commentator on Eric Voegelin, East had left the world of scholarship to run for the Senate.

Beside a political base that can be periodically activated, there is another characteristic that marks the Old Right as a social movement: a dedication to change. Genovese correctly notes that the Old Right addresses social issues in a frontal fashion. Unlike the neoconservatives, it remains irreconcilably opposed to the welfare state, feminism, and the principle of social equality. Unlike neoconservatives, moreover, the Old Right does not distinguish between moderate and radical feminism or between good and bad welfare states. The charge of Samuel T. Francis, an Old Right intellectual, leveled against the neoconservatives in the pages of *Modern Age,* of being the "harmless persuasion," may to some extent be justified from the standpoint of postwar conservatism. Neo-conservatives defend the status quo of corporate capitalism, the managerial state, modern women combining marriage and careers, and a civic religion of liberal democracy. The emphasis of Ben Wattenberg, Michael Ledeen, Joshua Muravchik, Peter L. Berger, and other neoconservatives on an activist foreign policy stems from their enthusiasm for contemporary America. In contrast, the Old Right, for all its professed anticommunism, retains some of its old isolationist spirit. The fear of entanglement runs deep in American history, and sociologist Irving Louis Horowitz has explained the elections of 1986 as an expression of content with Reagan's domestic policies but a rejection of a foreign policy that risks United States involvement in Central America.[7] Even more significantly, in contrast to first-generation traditionalists Russell Kirk, Robert A. Nisbet, and Thomas Molnar, the second generation of the Old Right does not blame perceived social ills on the weakness of government. It blames them on social engineers and bureaucrats who have seized power in the name of "affirmative" democratic government.

Nigel Ashford, the English political scientist, has observed a tendency among second-generation Old Rightists to advocate libertarian policies. Unlike libertarians, however, according to Ashford, the Old Right opposes the state not because of optimism about human nature, but because of hatred for a state apparatus that lies beyond their control. Despite the anarchist impulse perceptible among the Old Right, a less libertarian political strategy may also attract some of its members. New Right activists Richard Viguerie, Phyllis Schlafly, and Howard Phillips have grown impatient with the Reagan administration, which they accuse of abandoning a conservative social agenda for mere fiscal policy. Howard Phillips has also scolded the president and his advisors for turning against conservative allies in South Africa and Chile—in order to chase the will-o'-the-wisp of global democracy.[8]

The Old Right may be tempted to put off its war against the welfare state to join congenial New Rightists in support of a conservative social agenda. This Genovese sees as the bond uniting the two sides: laws against abortion and pornography and a counteroffensive against the gay and feminist lobbies. What renders this scenario unlikely is that those New Rightists who are still opposed to the neoconservatives are the same leaders whose foundations are foundering financially. How far can the Old Right go against the neoconservatives and the political left in alliance with the impoverished wing of the New Right? Equally significant is the question of how much headway the Old Right can make in joining libertarians to fight the welfare state. In either case the prospects for success are far from favorable.

The group on the Right that holds the good cards—money, journalistic clout, and administrative connections—are obviously the neoconservatives. However, to call them a social movement would be somewhat misleading. As Samuel Francis has argued, neoconservatism stands athwart any social movement on the Right that threatens welfare-capitalism and the managerial state.

Though a rightist social movement might not in any case have achieved either national dominance or cultural respectability, the neoconservatives have weakened and defunded whatever rightist challenge to the status quo had existed. And they did this while vigorously defending postwar America against the Left. Neoconservatives have made conservatism synonymous in people's minds with a defense of democratic capitalism and global democracy, against the critics of both whether on the Left or on the Right. This distinction in classification is sometimes slighted by neoconservatives in lumping together the radical Left and the radical Right as the protean enemy of American democracy. For example, both *Commentary* and the *Wall Street Journal* have made the improbable assertion that the German Greens have a right-wing nationalist character and membership.[9] The designated enemy of the neoconservatives is no longer, as in the 1970s, primarily the counterculture. Neoconservatives are fighting against the opposition to the America of the 1980s as defenders of the established order. Because they have fashioned the rhetoric and some of the policies of the Reagan administration, they are inevitably compelled to defend their own reputations.

For all these reasons, the group within postwar conservatism with the most power and prestige is both the least conservative and the least like a social movement. Leftist and Old Right critics remind us that the neoconservatives lack a genuine political base, save for those corporation heads who feather their foundational nests. Sidney Blumenthal makes this general point, although with little documentation in *The Rise of the Counterestablishment.* However, Arthur Hertzberg, in the *New York Review of Books,* proceeds in workmanlike fashion to show how surprisingly small is the neoconservatives' following. Their oft repeated claim to be the icebreaker of an American Jewish realignment with the Republican party and with the right center has turned out to be empty. In 1984, despite the support that neoconservative publications gave to the Reagan administration, the share of the Jewish vote received by the Republicans was less than in 1980. Moreover, Hertzberg contends, the 20 or so percent of the Jewish vote that went to Reagan came from groups whose voting behavior could not be plausibly attributed to neoconservative directives. Orthodox Jews and conventionally Republican German Jews voted for the political Right, without being under the sway of the *Commentary* circle.[10]

The neoconservatives' critics often fail to realize that their success has not been related to their being mistaken for a social movement. Francis makes the observation sarcastically in a review of Irving Kristol's partly autobiographical *Reflections of a Neoconservative,* but he is correct that neoconservatives have succeeded to some degree by appearing "harmless."[11] Most Americans, including many self-described conservatives, do not want a social movement on the Right. The combination of centrist politics at home and warnings against extremism characteristic of neoconservative polemicists suit well those corporate executives who subsidize their projects. In the 19 December 1986 *Wall Street Journal,* Suzanne Garment ends a discussion of expanding neoconservative think-tanks in Washington by listing the themes they address. These themes—smaller government, work and family, and strong defense—were and still are important to the Old Right. But Garment, who has often expressed her distaste for the pre-neoconservative Right, hastens to assure the reader: "But note the list is quite concrete. It is not put together simply to overturn the established order. It does not reek of general resentment against a ruling liberal establishment. It is the kind of list produced by people who directly or at one remove know something of governing—people who have in a sense arrived." Such tropes may infuriate theorists on both sides of the spectrum who dream of cataclysmic change, but they are reassuring to the respectable supporters of many conservative enterprises.

The lack of a social base may, however, hurt the neoconservatives in coping with two situations. One is an activist foreign policy that links anticommunism to global democracy and whose practitioners have been damaged by their involvement in recent embarrassing disclosures about the Reagan administration. The tight connections between neoconservatives and some foreign governments, particularly Israel, have already aroused bitter feelings against them. The suggestion that some neoconservatives, like Michael Ledeen, have had improper dealings with foreign governments will inevitably add to the suspicion about neoconservative adventurousness the even more damning charge (among Americans) of personal corruption, even though the charges have an obvious political motivation. Without a broad social or political movement behind them, neoconservatives may suffer as a group from the crisis of confidence that the press has begun to call "Iran-gate."

Without solid popular backing, the neoconservatives will also be unable to resist satellization or destruction by other groups of free-floating intellectuals. The neoliberalism of Lester Thurow and editorial boards of the *New Republic* and the *Washington Monthly* may prove appealing to left-wing neoconservatives, especially if linked to a triumphant Democratic administration. The combination of welfare state capitalism and an activist foreign policy which the neoconservatives advocate can become the keystone of a center left politics, without McGovernite rhetoric. The Coalition for a Democratic Majority, which Ben Wattenberg, Penn Kemble, Max Kampelman, Nathan Glazer, and other neoconservatives back and which claims to represent the Scoop Jackson or "Cold War liberal" tradition of the Democratic party, may be a bridge in more than one direction. The CDM may serve to lead neoconservatives back into the Democratic party as it once did into the Reagan camp. The prodigal sons will likely return if Charles Robb, Sam Nunn, or Bill Bradley, all perceived as acceptable moderates by most neoconservatives, is the Democrats' presidential nominee in 1988.[12]

It may be wrong to assume, like Genovese, that the waning of neoconservatism will bring to power an Old Right with a social base and theoretical foundation. Genovese's observation reflects his own admiration for Old Right theorists and historians who like himself examine "the dynamics of capitalism." He may also be led by his Marxist world view into looking for an authentic social movement to take the place of the neoconservatives as the dominant force on the Right. But unless the Old Right gains visibility and resources to win back its straying followers and to find new constituencies, it will not play the successor role to what might be the faltering neoconservatives.

Before giving in to anything like despair, conservatives in the 1980s might take considerable comfort from contemplating their forty-year rise to power. During the period, institutions rose and fell, leaders came to the fore and fell by the way; old friends and allies became bitter enemies; and yet some changes were made, some impact was had upon the American experience. Several powerful institutions—*National Review* and the Heritage Foundation—had demonstrated their staying power as well as the ability to adjust to changing times. However much doctrines may have altered, the fact remains that by the 1980s a great many Americans, perhaps more than at any other time, were willing to identify themselves as "conservative." That, in itself, may be the most enduring accompaniment of the postwar conservative movement.

Notes and References

Preface

1. "Symposium: How Has the United States Met Its Major Challenges Since 1945?" *Commentary* 80 (November 1985):37.

2. Ibid., 30.

3. See Robert Nisbet, *Conservatism* (Minneapolis: University of Minnesota Press, 1986), 25.

4. Aristotle, *Politica* I, 1260a, 20–24.

5. Although some of Aristotle's interpreters—for example, George Sabine and, more recently, Henry Jaffa—present him as a forerunner of modern democratic thinking, their work has usually included a highly selective reading of the *Politics,* particularly the middle books. Classical philologists and historians are less likely to pursue such a line of interpretation. See, for example, Sir David Ross, *Aristotle,* 4th ed. (London: Methuen, 1949). For a recent attempt to relate Aristotle's hierarchical view of the household and society to his understanding of nature, see Stephen R. L. Clark's essay in *Aristotle's Man* (Oxford: Oxford University Press, 1983), 99–113, and Wolfgang Kulman, "Equality in Aristotle's Political Thought," in *Equality and Inequality of Man in Ancient Thought,* ed. Iiro Kajanto (Helsinki, 1984), 372.

6. Alain de Benoist, *Vu de Droite* (Paris: Copernic, 1979), 18–26.

7. James Burnham, in *National Review,* 12 May 1972, 514.

8. See Wiliam F. Buckley, *American Conservative Thought in the Twentieth Century* (Indianapolis: Bobbs-Merrill, 1970), xv–xi; and the information about the J.B.S.'s precarious state in the *Baltimore Sun,* 15 September 1983.

9. Eric von Kuehnelt-Leddihn, in *Washington Times,* 18 November 1986, 3D.

10. James Burnham, in *National Review,* 12 May 1972, 516.

11. John Lukacs, *Outgrowing Democracy: A History of the United States in the Twentieth Century* (New York: Doubleday, 1984), 329.

12. Ibid., 330–41.

Chapter One

1. George H. Nash, *The Conservative Intellectual Movement in America since 1945* (New York: Basic Books, 1976), 4.

2. Mortimer Smith, "Individualism Talks Back," *Christian Century* 62 (February 14, 1945): 202.

3. Reported in *New York Times,* 2 August 1945, 1, 9.

4. H. S. Hughes, "Capitalism and History," *Commentary* 17 (1 April 1954):407.

5. For assessments of Hayek's significance as a social thinker by his disciples and erstwhile colleagues, see *Essays on Hayek,* ed. Fritz Machlup (New York: New York University Press, 1976). On the same subject, it may also be useful to read Lawrence K. Frank, "The Rising Stock of Dr. Hayek," *Saturday Review* 28 (12 May 1945):4–6; and Paul Gottfried, "The Road to Serfdom Revisited," *American Journal of Jurisprudence* 17 (1972):38–45.

6. William A. Rusher, *The Rise of the Right* (New York: William Morrow & Co., 1984), 33.

7. Quoted in John P. Diggins, *Up from Communism* (New York: Harper & Row, 1975), 344.

8. Rusher, *The Rise of the Right,* 42–44.

9. Whittaker Chambers, *Witness* (New York: Random House, 1952), 9.

10. See *The Gallup Poll,* vol. 2 (New York: Random House), 1220.

11. For a critical, impressionistic study of the effects of the cold war on American society and of the struggle itself, see John Lukacs, *A New History of the Cold War* (Garden City, N.Y.: Doubleday, 1966).

12. W. F. Buckley, Jr., and L. Brent Bozell, *McCarthy and His Enemies* (Chicago: Henry Regnery Co., 1954), 323.

13. James Burnham, in *National Review,* 1 June 1957, 518.

14. Frank Chodorov, *Out of Step: The Autobiography of an Individualist* (New York: Devin Adair, 1962). For Buckley's eulogy of Chodorov, see W. F. Buckley Jr., *The Jeweler's Eye* (New York: Putnam, 1968), 343–49.

15. See Diggins, *Up From Communism,* 326–29, for a study of Burnham's break with the Democratic Left, anticommunist American Committee for Cultural Freedom.

16. See, for example, Willmoore Kendall, "The Bill of Rights and American Freedom," in *What Is Conservatism?,* ed. Frank S. Meyer (New York: Holt, Rinehart, & Winston, 1964), 41–64.

17. As illustrations of Kendall's attempt to demonstrate the nonhistorical utopian character of the open society, see the posthumous anthology of his essays, *Willmoore Kendall Contra Mundum,* ed. Nellie D. Kendall (New Rochelle, N.Y.: Arlington House, 1971).

18. See especially Buckley, *McCarthy and His Enemies,* 308–40.

19. See *Protracted Conflict,* ed. Stefan Possony and Robert Strausz-Hupe (New York: Harper Colophon, 1963), and Stefan Possony, *A Century of Conflict:*

Communist Techniques of World Revolution (Chicago: Henry Regnery Co., 1953).

20. For a study of the European, particularly Hegelian, aspect of American conservative theory, see Paul Gottfried, *The Search for Historical Meaning: Hegel and the Postwar American Right* (DeKalb: Northern Illinois University Press, 1986).

21. Herbert J. Gans, *Popular Culture and High Culture* (New York: Basic Books, 1974), 54.

22. William F. Buckley, Jr., in *National Review,* 16 January 1962, 21.

23. Will Herberg, ibid., 10 April 1962, 250.

24. Editors, ibid., 24 August 1957, 149.

25. Jeffrey Hart, ibid., 18 June 1968, 604.

26. Frank Meyer, ibid., 4 October 1966, 998.

27. James Burnham, *Suicide of the West: An Essay on the Meaning and Destiny of Liberalism* (New Rochelle, N.Y.: Arlington House, 1964), 197–98.

28. See Richard Weaver, *Ideas Have Consequences* (Chicago: University of Chicago Press, 1948), particularly the introduction, and Bruce M. White, "Richard M. Weaver: Dialectic Rhetorician," *Modern Age* 26 (Summer–Fall 1982):256–59.

29. Rusher, *The Rise of the Right,* 28.

30. Two short appreciations of Kirk's work as a conservative theorist are Henry Regnery, "Russell Kirk and the Making of the Conservative Mind," *Modern Age* 21 (Fall 1977):338–53, and E. C. Kopff, "Russell Kirk: A Bohemian Tory," *Southern Partisan* 1 (Spring–Summer 1981):11-13.

31. Russell Kirk, *The Conservative Mind* (Chicago: Henry Regnery Co., 1953), 8.

32. Rusher, *The Rise of the Right,* 28–29.

33. See Russell Kirk's foreword to Peter J. Stanlis, *Edmund Burke and the Natural Law* (Ann Arbor: University of Michigan Press, 1958).

34. Two essays dealing with this shift of emphasis in Kirk's thinking are Donald Atwell Zoll, "The Social Thought of Russell Kirk," *Political Science Reviewer* 2 (Fall 1972):112–29, and W. Wesley McDonald, "Reason, Natural Law, and Moral Imagination in the Thought of Russell Kirk," *Modern Age* 27 (Winter 1983):15–24.

35. Kirk and Nisbet are both quoted on their intellectual debt to Nock in Nash, *The Conservative Intellectual Movement in America Since 1945,* 15.

36. Burke's modern critics as well as defenders have tried to find connections between his support of a market economy and his social traditionalism. See, for example, Michael Freeman, *Edmund Burke and the Critique of Political Radicalism* (Chicago: University of Chicago Press, 1980).

37. Meyer, "Freedom, Tradition, Conservatism," in *What Is Conservatism?,* 14.

38. Meyer's views on modern judicial activism are stated in a book by a close colleague that he helped inspire. See L. Brent Bozell, *The Warren Revo-*

lution: Reflections on the Consensus Society (New Rochelle, N.Y.: Arlington House, 1966).

39. M. Morton Auerbach, in *National Review,* 30 January 1962, 57.

40. Quoted in Russell Kirk, *T. S. Eliot and His Age,* 2nd ed. (LaSalle, Ill.: Sherwood Sugden & Co., 1984), 385.

41. Ibid.

42. Frank S. Meyer, "The Ballot in the Hand," *National Review,* 6 December 1958, 186.

43. Frank S. Meyer, in *National Review,* 16 May 1967, 527.

44. Ibid., 21 August 1968, 859.

45. Weaver, *Ideas Have Consequences,* vi.

46. Donald Davidson, *Still Rebels, Still Yankees* (Baton Rouge: Louisiana State University Press, 1957), 4–5.

Chapter Two

1. *U.S. News & World Report,* 20 July 1964, 41.

2. Ibid., 83.

3. S. M. Lipset and P. G. Altbach, "Student Politics and Higher Education in the United States," in *Student Politics,* ed., S. M. Lipset (New York: Basic Books, 1967), 219–20, and Richard G. Braungart, "SDS and YAF: Backgrounds of Student Political Activists" (mimeograph, Pennsylvania State University, Department of Sociology, 1966), 9–11.

4. W. F. Buckley, Jr., *God and Man at Yale* (Chicago: Henry Regnery Co., 1951), and Nash, *The Conservative Intellectual Movement in America Since 1945,* 376.

5. Taken from an interview with Larry Uzzell in Washington, D.C., October 1984.

6. Richard W. Flacks, "The Liberated Generation: An Exploration of the Roots of Student Protest," *Journal of Social Issues,* July 1967, 52–75; and Lawrence F. Schiff, "The Obedient Rebels: A Study of College Conversions to Conservatism," *Journal of Social Issues* 20 (October 1964):91, and "Conservatives on the Campus," *Newsweek,* 10 April 1961, 35.

7. See Samuel Lubell, "The People Speak" (news releases on student activism at Berkeley, 1966), 1–2, and S. Robert Lienters and Stanley Rothman's *Roots of Radicalism: Jews, Christians, and the New Left* (New York: Oxford University Press, 1982).

8. Braungart, "SDS and YAF," 38; see also Richard G. Braungart and David L. Westby, "Class and Politics in the Family Background of Student Political Activists," *American Sociological Review* 31 (1966):690–92.

9. M. Stanton Evans, *Revolt on the Campus* (Chicago: Henry Regnery Co., 1961), 68–70.

10. Lipset and Altbach, "Student Politics," 207.

11. *The Gallup Poll,* vol. 3 (1959–71), 129–93, 1479–80, 1912–13.

12. Ibid., vol. 2 (1949–58), 1201–2, 1220–21.

13. Ibid., vol. 3: 1784.

14. For the Declaration of Principles, see the appendix to J. Daniel Mahoney's *Actions Speak Louder: The History of the New York Conservative Party* (New Rochelle, N.Y.: Arlington House, 1968), 376–81.

15. *The Gallup Poll,* 3: 1772, 1785; and Andrew Greeley and Peter Rossi, *The Education of Catholic Americans* (Chicago, 1966).

16. For a provocative interpretation of these data, see Kevin P. Phillips, *The Emerging Republican Majority* (New Rochelle, N.Y.: Arlington House, 1969), 168.

17. William A. Rusher, "Crossroads for the GOP," *National Review,* 12 February 1963, 109–12. A short incisive critique of Rusher's underlying assumptions is available in Nelson Polsby and Aaron Wildavsky, *Presidential Elections,* 4th ed. (New York: Scribners, 1984), 161.

18. See Phillips, *The Emerging Republican Majority,* especially 458–60.

19. F. Clifton White, *Suite 3505: The Story of the Draft Goldwater Movement* (New Rochelle, N.Y.: Arlington House, 1967), especially the epilogue; and Rusher, *The Rise of the Right,* 159.

20. White, *Suite 3505,* 409.

21. Ibid., 413.

22. Craig Schiller, *The (Guilty) Conscience of a Conservative* (New Rochelle, N.Y.: Arlington House, 1978), 122–25. For a more conventional—that is, left-of-center—critique of the Goldwater campaign, see Richard Rovere, "The Conservative Mindlessness," *Commentary* 39 (March 1965):38.

23. Phillips, *The Emerging Republican Majority,* 166.

24. *The Gallup Poll,* 3:1917–18.

25. See Rusher, *The Rise of the Right,* 291–321, and M. Stanton Evans, *The Future of Conservatism: From Taft to Reagan and Beyond* (New York: Holt, Rinehart, & Winston, 1968). Although Evans's attempt to plot the upward course of postwar conservatism ends in 1968, he presents Reagan as presidential timber—and as the authentic heir of the political philosophy of Robert Taft and Barry Goldwater. Evans's work can be interpreted as a plea addressed to conservatives and Republicans to rally around Reagan as a presidential candidate—in preference to Goldwater's candidate, Richard Nixon.

26. Barry Goldwater, *The Conscience of a Conservative* (Shepherdsville, Ky.: Victor Publishing Co., 1960), 10–11.

27. William Rusher, in *The Rise of the Right,* 155, describes "Goldwater shying away from the very insight [conservatism] that made his candidacy different from any other. At heart Goldwater was, and remains, a perfectly orthodox, budget-balancing, main-line Republican, whose heart beats in near accord with Jerry Ford's." In view of Rusher's formative role in promoting Goldwater as a "conservative" presidential candidate, this judgment is truly damning.

28. See James Burnham, "Must Conservatives Be Republicans," *National Review*, 1 December 1964, 652.

29. For the 1964 Republican Presidential Platform, see *U.S. News & World Report*, 20 July 1964, 35.

30. This platform is given in Meyer's essay in *Left, Right, and Center*, ed. R. A. Goldwin (Chicago: Rand-McNally, 1965), 9–10.

31. See Barry Goldwater's plea to conservatives to support Nixon over Wallace in the *National Review*, 22 October, 1968, 1060–62.

32. Patrick Buchanan, *Conservative Votes, Liberal Victories* (New York: Quadrangle, 1975).

33. Rusher, *The Rise of the Right*, 263–90.

34. Meyer comments on the NYCP in the *National Review*, 3 July 1962, 486.

35. See the concluding chapter of Mahoney, *Actions Speak Louder.*

36. A point that Phillips disregards, but that Liberal Catholic Andrew Greeley stresses, is that Catholics usually gave nonconservative responses to social and economic questions in answering polls in the 1960s. (Abortion, birth control, and aid to parochial schools were consistent exceptions.) In October 1968 only 12 percent of Catholics expressed support for George Wallace. The same Gallup Poll had Wallace's Protestant support at 25 percent. See *The Gallup Poll*, 2:2166. Although many Catholics may have voted for Wallace without admitting it, it was obviously not something they were proud of. It expressed resentment far more than moral conviction. Nor was this hidden Catholic support for Wallace related to a publicly professed worldview, as it was among many Southern traditionalists.

37. See, for example, Jack Kemp, "Democratic Equality: A Conservative Idea?," *Intercollegiate Review* 20 (Spring–Summer 1985):51–56.

Chapter Three

1. Seymour Martin Lipset and David Riesman, *Education and Politics at Harvard* (New York: McGraw-Hill, 1975), 203.

2. Evans, *Revolt on Campus.*

3. Allan C. Carlson, "Luce, Life, and 'The American Way,' " *This World*, Winter 1986, 56–74.

4. Everett Carll Ladd, Jr., and Seymour Martin Lipset, *Academics, Politics, and the 1972 Election* (Washington, D.C.: AEI Domestic Affairs Studies, 1973), 2, 5ff.

5. Michael Lerner, "Respectable Bigotry," *American Scholar*, Autumn 1965, 606–17.

6. Lipset and Riesman, *Education*, 230.

7. *Freedom and Order in the University*, ed. Samuel Gorovitz (Cleveland: Press of Western Reserve University, 1967), 89ff.

8. George F. Kennan, *Democracy and the Student Left* (Boston: Little Brown, 1968).

9. Russell Kirk, *Decadance and Renewal in the Higher Learning* (South Bend, Ind.: Gateway, 1978), 23–24.

10. Jacques Barzun, *The House of Intellect* (1959; reprint, New York: Harper Torchback, 1961), 100.

11. Quoted in Albert Jay Nock, *The Theory of Education in the United States* (1932; reprint, New York: Arno Press, 1969).

12. Kirk, *Decadence,* 113.

13. *Against Mediocrity: The Humanities in America's High Schools,* ed. Chester E. Finn, Jr., Diane Ravitch, and Robert T. Fancher (New York: Holmes & Meier, 1984), 241ff.

14. Adam B. Ulam, "Where Do We Go From Here?" *Daedalus,* Fall 1974, 80–84.

15. Clark Kerr, *The Uses of the University* (Cambridge, Mass.: Harvard University Press, 1963).

16. Edward Gross and Paul V. Grambsh, *University Goals and Academic Power* (Washington, D.C.: American Council on Education, 1968).

17. Derek Bok, "On the Purpose of Undergraduate Education," *Daedalus,* Fall 1974, 159–72.

18. Jerry Farber, *The Student as Nigger* (New York: Contact Books, 1969).

19. Carl R. Rogers, "The Person of Tomorrow," 1969 commencement address at Sonoma State College.

20. Gerald F. Else, "Some Ill-Tempered Reflections on the Present State of Higher Education in the United States," *Daedalus,* Fall 1974, 138–42.

21. John A. Howard and Bruce Franklin, *Who Should Run the Universities?* (Washington, D.C.: American Enterprise Institute), 4ff.

22. Wayne C. Booth, *Now Don't Try to Reason with Me: Essays and Ironies for a Credulous Age* (Chicago: University of Chicago Press, 1970), 173.

23. Robert H. Bork, Howard C. Krane, and George D. Krane, *Political Activities of Colleges and Universities: Some Policy and Legal Implications* (Washington, D.C.: American Enterprise Institute, 1970).

24. Robert Wood, "Academe Sings the Blues," *Daedalus,* Winter 1975, 45–55.

25. For a survey, see Howard Gardner, *The Mind's New Science: A History of the Cognitive Revolution* (New York: Basic Books, 1985); see also Owen J. Flanagan, Jr., *The Science of the Mind* (Cambridge, Mass.: MIT Press, 1984).

26. Noam Chomsky, in *Language* 35 (1959):26–58.

27. See the discussion in Flanagan, *The Science of Mind,* 138ff., and Jerry Fodor, *The Language of Thought* (Cambridge, Mass.: Harvard University Press, 1979).

28. Brent Berlin and Paul Kay, *Basic Color Terms: Their Universality and Evolution* (Berkeley: University of California Press, 1969).

29. See Daniel G. Friedman, *Human Infancy: An Evolutionary Perspective*

(Hillsdale, N.J.: Halsted Press, 1974), and Peter C. Reynolds, *On the Evolution of Human Behavior: The Argument From Animals to Man* (Berkeley, Calif.: University of California Press, 1981).

30. See especially Charles J. Lumsden and Edward O. Wilson, *Promethean Fire: Reflections on the Origin of Mind* (Cambridge, Mass.: Harvard University Press, 1983).

31. Edward O. Wilson, *Sociobiology: The New Synthesis* (Cambridge, Mass.: Harvard University Press, 1975), and *On Human Nature* (Cambridge, Mass.: Harvard University Press, 1978).

32. See, for example, E. E. Maccoby and C. N. Jacklin, *The Psychology of Sex Differences* (Stanford, Calif.: Stanford University Press, 1974); Camilla P. Benbow and Julian C. Stanley, "Sex Differences in Mathematical Ability: Factor or Artifact?," *Science* 210 (1980):1261–64; and Melvin Konner, *The Tangled Wing: Biological Constraints on the Human Spirit* (New York: Holt, Rinehart, & Winston, 1982).

33. See the classic work of G. P. Murdock, *Social Structure* (New York: Macmillan, 1949); William N. Stephens, *The Family in Cross-Cultural Perspective* (New York: Holt, Rinehart, & Winston, 1963); and B. B. Whiting, *Six Cultures: Studies and Child Rearing* (New York: Wiley, 1963).

34. Sherry B. Ortner, "Is Female to Male as Nature Is to Culture?," in *Women, Culture, and Society,* ed. M. Z. Rosaldo and L. Lamphere (Stanford, Calif.: Stanford University Press, 1974), 67–68.

35. See especially Carol Gilligan, *In a Different Voice: Psychological Theory of Women's Development* (Cambridge, Mass.: Harvard University Press, 1982).

36. Leah Fritz, *Dreamers & Dealers: An Intimate Appraisal of the Women's Movement* (Boston: Beacon Press, 1979).

37. Lenore Weitzman, *The Divorce Revolution: The Unexpected Social and Economic Consequences for Women and Children in America* (New York: Free Press, 1986).

38. Martin Daly and Margo Wilson, "Child Abuse and Other Risks of Not Living with Both Parents," *Journal of Ethology Sociobiology* 6 (1985):197–210.

39. Steven Goldberg, *The Inevitability of Patriarchy* (New York: William Morrow, 1973), 233–34.

40. George Gilder, *Sexual Suicide* (New York: Quadrangle/New York Times Book Co., 1973).

41. R. C. Lewontin, Steven Rose, and Leon J. Kamin, *Not in Our Genes: Biology, Ideology, and Human Nature* (New York: Pantheon Books, 1984), 273 n.

42. Thomas Molnar, "Ethology and Environmentalism: Man as Animal and Mechanism," *Intercollegiate Review,* Fall 1977, 25–43.

43. Paul Johnson, *Modern Times: The World from the Twenties to the Eighties* (New York: Harper & Row, 1983), 734.

44. George Homans, *Coming to My Senses* (New Brunswick, N.J.: Transaction Books, 1984).

45. See especially Talcott Parsons and Edward E. Bales, *Family Socialization and Interaction Process* (New York: Free Press, 1955).

46. Steven Stack, "The Effect of Religious Commitment on Suicide: A Cross-National Analysis," *Journal of Health and Social Behavior* 24 (1983):362–74.

47. Edward C. Banfield, *The Unheavenly City: The Nature and the Foundation of Our Urban Crisis* (Boston: Little Brown, 1968), 16–17.

48. Milton Friedman, *Capitalism and Freedom* (Chicago: University of Chicago Press, 1967).

49. Milton Friedman, *A Monetary History of the United States 1867–1960* (Princeton: Princeton University Press, 1963).

50. See Stigler's papers collected in *The Intellectual and the Marketplace* (Cambridge, Mass.: Harvard University Press, 1964); and *The Economist as Preacher and Other Essays* (Chicago: University of Chicago Press, 1984).

51. *Chronicles,* September 1985, 32–33.

Chapter Four

1. The two autobiographical works that treat these Bildungsjahre are Norman Podhoretz's *Making It* (New York: Harper Row, 1967) and *Breaking Ranks* (New York: Harper Row, 1979).

2. See "Counter Culture and Its Apologists," *Commentary* 50 (December 1970): 40–59.

3. See, for example, E. Raab, "Black Revolution and the Jewish Question," *Commentary* 47 (April 1969):6, and N. Glazer, "Blacks, Jews, and the Intellectuals," *Commentary* 47 (April 1969):33–39.

4. See Isidore Silver, "What Flows from Neoconservatism," *Nation,* 9 July 1977, 49, and Alexander Bloom, *Prodigal Sons* (New York: Oxford University Press, 1986).

5. For a perceptive but partisan interpretation of these data, see Arthur Hertzberg, "Reagan and the Jews," *New York Review of Books,* 31 January 1985, 11–14.

6. A discussion of American Jewish political and moral attitudes can be found in a symposium, "Jews and American Politics," in *This World* 10 (Winter 1985):4–38.

7. See John B. Judis, "The Conservative Wars," *New Republic,* 11 August 1986, 15–18; and George Archibald's report on the same topic on the front page of the *Washington Times,* 9, 16 June 1986.

8. For a clarification of Bradford's beliefs, see his *Remembering Who We Are: Observations of a Southern Conservative* (Athens: University of Georgia Press, 1985); and Paul Gottfried's investigation of that book and its critics, "Looking Back," *The World and I* 8 (August 1986):460–64.

9. See Sidney Blumenthal, *The Rise of the Counterestablishment: From*

Conservative Ideology to Political Power (New York: Times Books, 1986), especially 122–66.

10. Christopher Hitchens, "A Modern Medieval Family," *Mother Jones,* July 1986, 52–56; August 1986, 74–76.

11. See Jeane Kirkpatrick, "Dictatorships and Double Standards," *Commentary* 68 (November 1979):34–45; and Alexander Bloom, *Prodigal Sons,* 370–71.

12. This Bicentennial issue of *Public Interest* was subsequently published as *The American Commonwealth,* ed. Nathaniel Glazer and Irving Kristol (New York, 1976).

13. For Glazer's critical comments about the evolution of the civil rights movement, see Nathan Glazer, "Blacks, Jews, and the Intellectuals," *Commentary* 47 (April 1969):35; and "The Limits of Social Policy," *Commentary* 52 (September 1971):51–58; "Is Busing Necessary?," *Commentary* 52 (March 1972):39–52. See also Banfield, *The Unheavenly City.*

14. See Edward Shapiro, "Conservatism and Its Discontents," *The World and I* 9 (September 1986):565–72.

15. See Irving Kristol, *Reflections of a Neoconservative: Looking Back, Looking Ahead* (New York: Basic Books, 1983), xii; and "The David I Knew," *Wall Street Journal,* 9 May 1986, 26.

16. See George Will, *Statecraft as Soulcraft: What Government Does* (New York: Simon & Schuster, 1983), 93–94.

17. See Allan Carlson's *Persuasion at Work,* 9 (August–September 1986); and Peter L. Berger's remarks in *Commentary* 80 (November 1985):30–31.

18. See Brigitte Berger and Peter L. Berger, *The War over the Family: Capturing the Middle Ground* (New York, 1983), for a telling critique of modern welfare state "family policy."

19. See George F. Gilder, "Still Different," *National Review,* 30 November 1984, 48–50.

20. See for example, Michael Ledeen, "How to Support the Democratic Revolution," *Commentary* 76 (March 1985):43–46; and Carnes Lord, "In Defense of Public Diplomacy," *Commentary* 77 (April 1984):42–50.

21. Podhoretz, *Breaking Ranks,* 356–58.

22. Diane Ravitch, "The Precarious State of History," *American Educator,* Spring 1985, 10–17.

23. See Suzanne Garment's column in the *Wall Street Journal,* 11 October 1985, 26.

24. In *The Rise of the Counterestablishment,* 151–54, Sidney Blumenthal takes seriously the assertions made in *Reflections of a Neoconservative* and elsewhere about Kristol's Straussian attachments. Blumenthal goes so far as to interpret Kristol's political theory on the basis of them.

25. For a representative tribute to Lionel Trilling by a moderately conservative Jewish follower, see Steven Marcus, "Lionel Trilling 1905–1975," *New York Times Book Review,* 8 February 1976, 32–34. See also Podhoretz, *Breaking*

Ranks, 296–300; and Mark Krupnick, *Lionel Trilling and Cultural Criticism in America* (Evanston: Northwestern University Press, 1986).

26. Bloom, *Prodigal Sons,* 37–39.

27. The view that the individual is morally and emotionally dependent upon community identity and firmly established tradition is an *idée maîtresse* in the writings of Robert Nisbet. His most recent book, *Conservatism* (Minneapolis: University of Minnesota, 1986), is a summing-up of his entire conservative social theory.

28. See *Intercollegiate Review* 21 (Spring 1986):66.

29. Two interesting accounts of the heated exchanges that occurred at the Philadelphia Society, one sympathetic to the neoconservatives and the other written from a moderate leftist perspective, are Jeffrey Hart, "Conservative Warfare in Chicago," *National Review,* 6 June 1986, 32–34, and John B. Judis, "The Conservative Mental Breakdown," *New Republic,* 1 August 1986, 15–18. On the same subject, see also Paul Gottfried, "Editorial Notes," *Continuity* 10 (Spring 1985):i–iii.

30. See Gillian Peele, *Revival and Reaction: The Right in Contemporary America* (Oxford: Clarendon Press, 1904), 1–51, and Gregory Wolfe, *Right Mind: A Source Book of American Conservative Thought* (Chicago: Regnery/Gateway, 1986), for a survey of conservative and neoconservative think tanks and celebrities. For a demonological but comprehensive view of the same subject, see John S. Saloma III, *Ominous Politics: The New Conservative Labyrinth* (New York: Hill & Wang, 1983), 7–37.

31. Representative of the neoconservative view of McCarthy and McCarthyism is Joseph Bishop, "The End of Senator Joe McCarthy," in the neoconservative *American Spectator* 16 (December 1983):16–20. The same issue features a drawing of Senator McCarthy sitting in a garbage can covered with litter.

32. See the information on AEI in *Insight,* 7 April 1986, 26–27 and 21 July 1986, 21; and "A Thinktank at the Brink," *Newsweek,* 7 July 1986, 67.

33. In conversation with one of the authors on 28 July 1986.

Chapter Five

1. Peele, *Revival,* 52.

2. James C. Roberts, *The Conservative Decade: Emerging Leaders of the 1980's* (Westport, Conn.: Arlington House, 1980), 7.

3. Richard A. Viguerie, *The New Right: We're Ready to Lead* (Falls Church, Va.: Viguerie Co., 1980), 54–55.

4. Alan Crawford, *Thunder on the Right: The "New Right" and the Politics of Resentment* (New York: Pantheon, 1980).

5. John S. Saloma III, *Ominous Politics: The New Conservative Labyrinth* (New York: Hill & Wang, 1984), 46ff.

6. Peele, *Revival,* 67–68.

7. Dinesh D'Souza, *Falwell Before the Millennium: A Critical Biography* (Chicago: Regnery/Gateway, 1984), 97.

8. Ibid., 151.

9. Stuart Rothenberg and Frank Newport, *The Evangelical Voter: Religion and Politics in America* (Washington, D.C.: Free Congress Research & Education Foundation, 1984), 133.

10. Kenneth Wald, *Religion & Politics in the United States* (New York: St. Martin's Press, 1987), 205.

11. Linda Metcalf and Kenneth Dolbeare, *Neopolitics: American Political Ideas in the 1980's* (Philadelphia: Temple University Press, 1985), 165.

12. *Whose Values?: The Battle for Morality in Pluralistic America,* ed. Carl Horn (Ann Arbor, Mich.: Servant Books, 1985), 183.

13. George Gilder, "Sexual Politics," *Chronicles,* June 1986, 10.

14. See *Phyllis Schlafly Report* 13, no. 1 (1979).

15. Joseph Sobran, *Single Issues* (New York: Human Life Press, 1983), 16.

16. See Joseph Scheidler, *Closed: 99 Ways to Stop Abortion* (Westchester, Ill.: Crossway Books, 1985).

17. See, for example, *Persuasion at Work,* January, August, September, November 1985.

18. Mary Pride, *The Child Abuse Industry: Outrageous Facts and Everday Rebellions Against a System That Threatens Every North American Family* (Westchester, Ill.: Crossway Books, 1986).

19. John Whitehead, *Parents' Rights* (Westchester, Ill.: Crossway Books, 1985).

20. Phyllis Schlafly, ed., *Child Abuse in the Classroom* (Alton, Ill.: Pere Marquette Press, 1984).

21. Paul Vitz, *Censorship: Evidence of Lies in Our Children's Textbooks* (Ann Arbor, Mich.: Servant Books, 1986), 60.

22. Ibid., 75.

23. Viguerie, *New Right,* 77–78.

24. See *Grass Roots: The Leadership Quarterly of the Conservative Caucus,* December 1985–January 1986.

25. *The New Right Papers,* ed. Robert W. Whitaker (New York: St. Martin's Press, 1982).

26. Ibid., 106–27.

27. Ibid., 180–200.

28. Ibid., 123–24.

29. Ibid., 200.

30. Ibid., 64–83.

31. Ibid., 80.

32. "Louder Thunder on the Right," *Fortune* 23 (January 1984):36–37.

33. Richard Viguerie, in *National Review,* 19 October 1984.

34. See David Brooks, "Please, Mr. Postman: The Travails of Richard Viguerie," *National Review,* 20 June 1986, 28–32.

35. William S. Lind, "What is Cultural Conservatism," *Essays on Our Times,* March 1986.

36. Chester Finn, "Giving Shape to Cultural Conservatism," *American Spectator,* November 1986, 14–16.

Chapter Six

1. Revilo P. Oliver, *America's Decline: The Education of a Conservative* (London: Londinium Press, 1981), 153ff.

2. In 1986 the *Nation* stirred up a continuing controversy by publishing and defending an exotically anti-Zionist article by novelist Gore Vidal.

3. Kevin P. Phillips, *Post-Conservative America: People, Politics, and Ideology in a Time of Crisis* (New York: Random House, 1982).

4. See "Fighting for a Slice of the Apple Pie," *U.S. News & World Report,* 24 November 1986, 25.

5. See Donald J. Devine, *Reagan Electionomics 1976–1984* (Ottawa, Ill.: Green Hill Publishers, 1983).

6. Eugene Genovese, in *New Republic,* 29 December 1986, 39–40.

7. Irving Louis Horowitz, *Chronicles: A Magazine of American Culture,* February 1987, 17–18.

8. Extended interview with Howard Phillips, 30 December 1986.

9. See, for example, David Gress, "What the West Should Know about German Neutralism," *Commentary* 75 (January 1983):26–31.

10. Arthur Hertzberg, "Reagan and the Jews," *New York Review of Books,* 31 January 1985, 11–14.

11. See Samuel T. Francis's review of Irving Kristol's *Reflections of a Neoconservative, Modern Age* 29 (Winter 1985):76–79.

12. See Ben Wattenberg's remarks in "Nunn or Robb or Neither," *Washington Times,* 18 December 1986, DI.

Bibliographic Essay

Among the general surveys on postwar American conservatism, the most comprehensive and best known is George H. Nash, *The Conservative Intellectual Movement Since 1945* (New York: Basic Books, 1976). Other less detailed and certainly more subjective accounts of the conservative movement are Clinton Rossiter, *Conservatism in America: The Thankless Persuasion* (New York: Viking, 1962); *National Review* editor Jeffrey Hart, *The American Dissent* (New York: Doubleday, 1966); John P. Diggins, *Up From Communism* (New York: Harper & Row, 1975); Gillian Peele, *Revival and Reaction: The Right in Contemporary America* (Oxford: Clarendon Press, 1984)—a valuable perspective by an English liberal; William A. Rusher, *The Rise of the Right* (New York: William Morrow & Co., 1984)—a personal account by one of the key figures; and Sidney Blumenthal, *The Rise of Counterestablishment: From Conservative Ideology to Political Power* (New York: Times Books, 1986)—an inaccurate, biased but sometimes insightful essay by a *Washington Post* political reporter.

Books that represent particular streams of American conservatism are Russell Kirk, *The Conservative Mind: From Burke to Eliot,* 7th ed. (Chicago: Regnery Books, 1986)—arguably the most influential conservative book written after World War II; Irving Kristol, *Two Cheers for Capitalism* (New York: Basic Books, 1978)—a classic work of neoconservative analysis; and Robert A. Nisbet, *Conservatism* (Minneapolis: University of Minnesota Press, 1986). For works that continue to exemplify the southern agrarian spirit, see Clyde N. Wilson, ed., *Why the South Will Survive* (Athens: University of Georgia Press, 1981), and Melvin E. Bradford, *Remembering Who We Are* (Athens: University of Georgia Press, 1985). As examples of Old Right intellectual analysis, see Claes G. Ryn, *Democracy and the Ethical Life* (Baton Rouge: Louisiana State University Press, 1978), and Paul Gottfried, *The Search for Historical Meaning: Hegel and the Postwar American Right* (DeKalb: Northern Illinois University Press, 1986). The best conservative interpretation of the Constitution is given by Forrest McDonald, *Novus Ordo Seclorum: The Intellectual Origins of the Constitution* (Lawrence: University Press of Kansas: 1985). For a popular exercise in pure capitalism, see Milton and Rose Friedman, *The Tyranny of the Status Quo* (New York: Harcourt Brace Jovanovich, 1984); Charles Murray, *Losing Ground: American Social Policy, 1950–1980* (New York: Basic, 1984); George Gilder, *The Spirit of Enterprise* (New York: Simon & Schuster, 1984); Michael Novak, *The Spirit of Democratic Capitalism* (New York: Simon & Schuster, 1982); and Robert Bork, *The Antitrust Paradox: A Policy at War With Itself* (New York: Basic, 1980). Finally, the populist strain is exemplifed in Robert W. Whitaker, ed., *The New Right Papers* (New York: St. Martin's Press, 1982), and Kevin P. Phillips, *Post-Conservative America: People, Politics and Ideology in a Time of Crisis* (New York: Random House, 1982).

Works written since 1945 that have profoundly affected American conservative thought are Friedrich Hayek, *The Road To Serfdom,* 17th ed. (Chicago: Phoenix Books, 1963); Whittaker Chambers, *Witness* (New York: Random House, 1952); Robert A. Nisbet, *The Quest for Community* (Oxford: Oxford University Press, 1953); Richard M. Weaver, *Ideas Have Consequences* (Chicago: Phoenix Books, 1948); Eric Voegelin, *The New Science of Politics* (Chicago: Phoenix Books, 1952); Leo Strauss, *Natural Right and History* (Chicago: Phoenix Books, 1965); C. Brent Bozell and William Buckley, *McCarthy and His Enemies* (Chicago: Regnery, 1954); Willmoore Kendall, *The Conservative Affirmation* (Chicago: Regnery, 1962); Thomas Molnar, *The Decline of the Intellectual* (New York: Meridian Books, 1962); Franks S. Meyer, *In Defense of Freedom* (Chicago: Regnery, 1962); James Burnham, *Suicide of the West: An Essay on the Meaning and Destiny of Liberalism* (New York: John Day, 1964); Edward C. Banfield, *The Unheavenly City: The Nature and the Foundation of Our Urban Crisis* (Boston: Little, Brown & Co., 1970); and Norman Podhoretz, *Breaking Ranks* (New York: Harper & Row, 1979).

Index